DATE			

VM Performance
Management

VM Performance Management

Trevor Eddolls

Intertext Publications
McGraw-Hill Book Company

New York St. Louis San Francisco Auckland Bogotá
Hamburg London Madrid Mexico Milan Montreal
New Delhi Panama Paris São Paulo
Singapore Sidney Tokyo Toronto

Library of Congress Catalog Card Number 89-83770

ISBN 0-07-018966-8

Intertext Publications/Multiscience Press, Inc.
One Lincoln Plaza
New York, NY 10023

McGraw-Hill Publishing Company
1221 Avenue of the Americas
New York, NY 10020

Composed in Ventura Publisher by Context, Inc.

This book is dedicated to
Jill, Katy, and Jennifer

Contents

Acknowledgments

I would like to thank all the people at Xephon who facilitated the preparation and writing of this book, in particular Chris Bunyan and Steve Piggot. Without their help it would not have been possible.

I would also like to thank my family, Jill, Katy, and Jennifer, for all the things that they did and didn't do, so that I could get on with writing.

Foreword

Management of the performance of VM is becoming increasingly important because there is a growing number of sites installing VM and using it as a commercial system. *VM Performance Management* is intended to be a source of useful information and hints and tips for all people associated with the performance of the VM system. The author takes the view that the performance of the system can only be interpreted once all the components of the system and their interrelationship are understood. To this end, part of the book is taken up with explanatory text that attempts to at least give an overview of system components for those readers who may not be fully conversant with them. The book then looks in more detail at the areas where performance improvements could be made and suggests things to look for or ways that improvements to system performance might be made.

WHO THE BOOK IS FOR

The book is primarily intended for use by systems programmers who will be responsible for making any permanent changes to the way that the system performs. The book is also intended to be of use to operators and operations support staff who need to understand the system they are working on before they make any dynamic modifications to it. The third group for whom the book is intended are managers who need to gain an insight into how the system works and what their role is in managing VM performance.

The nontechnical reader is not excluded from this book and will find that many previously impenetrable areas of VM are explained, and a full glossary is provided to give extra help with this. They will find that this greater understanding is an asset not only in their own work, but also when dealing with the technical departments.

WHICH VM?

VM is not one uniform product, but comes in many versions from VM/IS to VM/XA SP. The book describes VM systems in general while taking great care to point out the differences, where they occur, between the different versions. In this way the book should be of use to people from sites with any version of VM, as well as those migrating from one version to another.

1

Introduction

With an estimated 22,000 VM licenses wordwide it is important for the companies who have installed the system to get the most out of it. Like any tool used by an organization it has cost money to install and costs money to run. Therefore, it is to the advantage of that organization for VM to run as effectively and efficiently as possible under all circumstances.

The purpose of this book is to explain the way VM works and to highlight those areas that would be worth examining in order to improve performance, and it examines the various aspects of performance management. The book is intended to give users some ideas of changes that they could make to the system and to subsystems, and also an idea of the consequences they can anticipate from any change. It should be borne in mind at all times that each system is unique in terms of hardware, software, and number of users, and will itself change with the passage of time. Therefore, be warned at the outset that there is no universal panacea for poor performance.

The first part of this chapter looks at the history of VM up to the present and examines briefly the different versions of VM available. The second part of the chapter looks at performance expectations and what is meant by performance management. The third part of this chapter summarizes the contents of the other chapters in the book, explaining their relevance and how they relate to each other.

VM HISTORY

VM was first developed in the mid-1960s at Cambridge, Massachusetts, as a way of giving each user the appearance of working on his *own* computer system. This meant that every user worked from his terminal (the console for his system) as if he had his own processor, unit record devices (i.e., printer, card reader, and card punch), and DASD. The VM Control Program (CP) would look after the real resources and allocate them as required by the users. The product was then called CP/40. At much the same time they were working on a user-friendly operating system called the Cambridge Monitor System (CMS).

The first commercial version of VM was called CP/67 and ran on the old 360/67 machine. In the early 1970s when the 370-architecture machines were introduced, a new version of VM called VM/370 became available. CMS by this time had retained its initials but changed its name to Conversational Monitor System, thus highlighting its interactive nature. The commercial product also included Remote Spooling Communication Subsystem (RSCS) and Interactive Problem Control System (IPCS), which ran under CMS.

In its early stages VM was not very popular and IBM did not market it with much vigor, preferring to sell DOS or VS1. There is a story that T. Vincent Learson, the IBM president at that time, watched a presentation from the MVS group that argued convincingly for VM to be axed. It was only after the presentation that Learson noticed that the MVS development team were themselves running MVS under VM. From then on VM became more of a feature in IBM marketing, and in 1979 became a fully supported product. This coincided with the introduction of the 4300 series of mainframes.

CURRENT SYSTEMS

At the moment there are five versions of VM available. These are:

- VM/IS
- VM/SP
- VM/SP HPO
- VM/XA SF
- VM/XA SP

There is another system expected, which is known as VM/ESA.

VM/IS

VM/IS is designed and marketed for users of low-end environments, primarily 9370s. It is a version of VM/SP which, it is claimed, can be installed without the aid of systems programming staff. Although this may be true, it is almost impossible to tune it without some systems programming knowledge. Associated with VM/IS are what are called SolutionPacs. These contain the required software to run the various parts (in addition to VM) necessary to have a working system. A user specifies the requirements and IBM sends a Solution-Pac with compatible releases of software to fit these requirements. It can be easily installed and is ready to run (according to IBM). VM/IS will support up to 16 MB of real storage and allows a maximum of 16 channels.

VM/SP

VM/SP is the basic VM system. It is aimed at intermediate environments and offers all the facilities associated with VM. VM/SP will also support up to 16 MB of real storage and support 16 channels. It was the first version to support the Shared File System (SFS) and AVS (APPC/VM VTAM Support), but does not support extended storage or cache DASD controllers.

VM/SP HPO

VM/SP HPO is the version of VM aimed at large performance-oriented environments. The High Performance Option is really compulsory if sites want to run high-performance guest systems, i.e., MVS/SP. VM/SP HPO will support up to 64 MB of real storage, although virtual machines are restricted to a maximum of 16 MB. HPO will support up to 32 channels and cache DASD controllers. Release 6 supports SFS. The demise of HPO has been predicted.

VM/XA SF

The SF version of VM/XA was aimed at large environments that wanted to run MVS/XA as a guest system. In almost all cases, to use the facilities of VM, e.g., CMS, it was necessary to install a second VM system as a guest under VM/XA.

VM/XA SP

VM/XA SP is currently the top of the range VM operating system. It is aimed at large environments that are running MVS/XA or MVS/ESA as a guest operating system. It contains most of the facilities available with VM/SP and VM/SP HPO. There is no requirement to run an additional VM guest system. It will support up to 2 GB of real storage and allows virtual machines to have up to 999 MB of virtual storage. It will support up to 3000 CMS machines.

USES

VM was initially sold as being useful in three 'niche' markets. These were:

- As a time sharing system for scientific and academic applications
- As a programmer development tool
- As a migration aid from one operating system to another

Currently, typical reasons for selecting and installing VM might also include:

- To run multiple guest operating systems
- To allow personal computing, e.g., CMS or APL
- To support Information Centers
- To support PROFS
- To support a guest operating system on hardware that will not support it running native (typically VSE systems)

PERFORMANCE EXPECTATIONS

Before any kind of performance tuning can be carried out, it is necessary to understand how the system works, including how the subsystems interrelate, and decide what criteria are to be applied and how much importance is to be attached to each virtual machine. This means that goals will have to be identified for system performance based on a number of factors. These include:

- Company needs
- Internal financing and fiscal policy

• Realistic service levels
• Hardware and system constraints

Company Needs

The company will have installed a mainframe processor with the intention of using it as a tool for making money. This is usually achieved by being able to speed up certain processes and make information available more quickly and easily to decision-making personnel. Therefore, the company will expect the performance of the system to enhance its position in business.

Internal Financing

One of the limiting factors on the system will be the availability of hardware and software. For example, performance can often be improved by installing a faster processor. This usually will cost the company money. It is necessary that the required amount of money be made available to ensure that the system will perform up to the company's requirements.

If a company is divided into a number of departments, each with its own internal budget that it uses to pay for the services of the data processing department, it may be necessary from time to time to review those budgets in the light of the amount of processing performed and to ensure that the performance of that department meets the company's standards.

Realistic Service Levels

The company as a whole must expect its data processing department to offer a realistic level of service. If it expects a system to be available 24 hours a day, 365 days a year, this is clearly unrealistic even with the more reliable systems available today. It leaves no time for installing new releases of system software, which require an IPL or other necessary maintenance activities.

It is important that users come to expect a level of service that the DP department can realistically provide. Typically a user's perception of system performance depends on terminal response times. If users experience a wide variation in response times, this will often result in them moaning about the service in general. It is usually found that users are satisfied with consistent response times even if they are nowhere near subsecond in length.

It is necessary that executive or management decisions are made as to which type of work is most important to the company. If a large CICS network is to be run under a guest system running under VM, then this should get a better service level. Providing this level of service may result in a reduction in the service available to CMS users and others.

Some kind of hierarchy must be established so that the performance expectations of virtual machines at the top of the hierarchy will be higher than the performance expectations of those at the bottom. Once this hierarchy is established, steps can be taken to ensure that the system works to those specifications and measurements can be made using some kind of monitor to ensure the criteria are satisfied. If they are not, then tuning can be carried out. Also, regular reviews should be held to ensure that the hierarchy still meets the company's needs. If not, it should be modified and the system tuned to meet the modified requirements.

Hardware and System Constraints

All the people concerned with VM must be made aware of the limitations placed on performance by the hardware and software selected.

Smaller and older machines will have slower throughput rates. A newer processor will usually improve performance by doing the same amount of work faster. Also, if more memory is installed, there is more room for virtual machines. Therefore, less time will be spent paging, and more work or improved performance can be achieved.

There are also constraints imposed by VM itself. SP can only use up to 16 MB of main memory, whereas HPO can use up to 64 MB. If more memory is available, then performance improvements could be achieved by upgrading to HPO.

Again, all upgrades carry an additional cost, which must be borne by the company. Sensible capacity planning can be used to ensure that all upgrades are budgeted for and installed before performance drops to unacceptable levels.

PERFORMANCE MANAGEMENT

Performance management at many sites is in the process of evolving from a technical activity, in many instances involved in "fire-fighting" techniques, to what is much more of a strategic issue. This new style performance management is made up of a series of tasks that each have to be carried out successfully and their interrelationship fully understood.

The components of performance management are:

- Understanding how the software works
- Understanding the requirements of the subsystems and applications being run and understanding their interdependencies
- Understanding the features and limitations associated with all hardware components in use
- Knowing what online changes can be made to the system
- Measuring system performance
- Monitoring system performance
- Reporting performance to people who need to know in a way that allows them to gain as much information as quickly as possible
- Tuning system components
- Estimating future system requirements (capacity planning) and taking steps to meet those needs.
- Coordinating capacity planning and application development functions
- Setting realistic service levels and ensuring that they are met
- Publicizing performance successes

"Fire-fighting" techniques tend to be associated with problem determination and trouble-shooting. In addition to the information presented in this book, areas that it would be useful for technical specialists to understand fully include:

- Software errors
- System loops
- System restarts
- CP and CMS commands for debugging
- The use of IPCS or DVF
- The use of CPTRAP and FRET trap

PERFORMANCE MANAGEMENT AND THIS BOOK

The other chapters in this book are designed to help with the various aspects of performance management.

Chapter 2 gives an overview of VM as a way of familiarizing the reader with VM's many facets, identifying what they are and why they are important. Some of these facets are dealt with in more detail in later chapters.

Chapter 3 describes in detail the way that virtual machines are processed by the control program. It is important to understand this, as many changes that are made to the system alter the way that virtual machines are selected for processing. The chapter explains how the dispatcher and scheduler work and looks at the different queues that are maintained. The calculation of the dispatching priority is explained.

Chapter 4 examines paging, describing how it works and the differences between the various VM systems. This is an area that is often responsible for performance problems and an understanding of how it works is essential to anyone planning to tune their system.

Chapter 5 looks at the various assists that are available on different models of processor and highlights what they are used for in terms of system or subsystem performance.

Chapter 6 describes those SET commands that can be used to dynamically modify the way the system is performing at any one time. The command format is given along with reasons for using the command, how the command works, what problems can be experienced when using the command, and solutions to these problems.

Chapter 7 takes a detailed look at the I/O subsystem examining both hardware and software aspects. Because paging, spooling, and data transfer to and from files use the I/O subsystem, it is important that it perform as efficiently as possible, and this chapter is full of hints and tips on improving the way it performs.

Chapter 8's area of focus is networks and communication software. With more and more sites using VTAM, network performance is becoming a major issue at many sites. The chapter describes the hodge-podge of software available in the communications area, including NetView; and also examines various aspects of network performance.

Chapter 9 takes a more detailed look at some of the subsystems that could be running under VM and looks at ways that their performance could be improved. Subsystems considered are: CMS, guest operating systems, CICS, SQL/DS, and PROFS.

Chapter 10 discusses performance monitors. It looks at what they could be used for and what types are available. The VM monitor is described, and many of the performance monitors currently available are briefly reviewed. Finally, a number of detailed questions are suggested that should be asked before a performance monitor is selected.

Chapter 11 considers performance reports describing various aspects of reporting, including what aspects of performance should be reported; who should get a copy of a report; how much information they require; how the information is to be reported; how often they want the report; and what the report is to be used for.

Chapter 12 takes an in-depth look at various aspects of tuning the system and capacity planning. It takes a detailed look at measuring the system and evaluating the results before any tuning or capacity planning work is performed. The last part of the chapter looks at various aspects of setting up the system or performing an upgrade.

These chapters are designed to give anyone plenty of information to help them with the process of performance management in a VM environment.

2

Overview of VM

This chapter is designed to give an appreciation of the various components of VM so that when they are discussed in more detail or referred to later in the text, the reader will be in a better position to understand the significance of the information.

The VM Control Program (CP) acts as a "hypervisor" and controls all the real hardware that is connected to the processor. It is made up of a number of software modules (discussed later). It provides the environment for the virtual machines to exist and also supplies facilities to allow them to communicate.

Running under VM are any number of virtual machines. Each virtual machine must have an entry in the system directory. This entry will specify the apparent hardware environment for that virtual machine; i.e., it will identify disks, printers, and card readers, etc., and it will also specify the virtual machine's apparent real storage size.

Some virtual machines are run disconnected. This means that they do not have a console (terminal) connected to them. SMART (the online monitor) and RSCS (the remote spooling system) both typically run disconnected.

Some virtual machines are called service machines because they provide particular services to other virtual machines. An example of a service machine is SQL/DS.

Usually the majority of virtual machines running under VM are CMS machines. CMS is an operating system that offers users very good interactive facilities. Many program products are designed to

CP						
CMS	CMS	CMS	RSCS	SQL/DS	MVS	VSE

Figure 2-1   System set-up.

run under CMS, e.g., XEDIT, COBOL, PL/I, IPCS, PROFS, and SQL/DS.

A guest operating system, e.g., MVS or VSE, may also execute under VM. The guest system will process in the usual way, allowing multiprogramming, etc. It is possible to run two or more guest systems under VM at the same time. It is also possible to run VM under VM.

An example of the arrangement of CP and virtual machines is illustrated in Figure 2-1.

VM COMPONENTS

The components of a working VM system would include some or all of the following:

- Control Program (CP)—the heart of the system.
- Conversational Monitor System (CMS)—an operating system used to maintain the system components, to provide end-user computing, and for program development. PROFS, SQL/DS, and CICS/VM all run under CMS.
- Remote Spooling Communication Subsystem (RSCS)—allows spool files to be sent to remote users or other spooling systems, e.g., JES2.
- Interactive Problem Control System (IPCS)—used for problem analysis and runs under CMS. It has been superseded on XA systems by Dump Viewing Facility (DVF).
- VM Real-Time Monitor—an online monitor that reports on any exception conditions. It is better known by its run time name of SMART.
- VMMAP—a historical monitor and reporting tool.

- Group Control System (GCS)—a very basic operating system that runs under CP and supports VTAM and VTAM applications, e.g., RSCS or NetView.
- Passthrough—sometimes known as PVM, it allows terminals to access other systems and, indirectly, SNA networks.

Some other frequently encountered software products are:

- ISPF
- PROFS
- SQL/DS
- TSAF

PROCESSOR STATES

When the processor is performing instructions, it is described as being in one of two states:

- Supervisor state
- Problem state

Supervisor State

When CP is using the processor to perform activities such as paging or managing I/O, it is described as being in supervisor state. Because CP is active, the virtual machines that it supports are not active. This can be considered as an overhead for the systems running under CP.

Problem State

Problem state is the name given to the state that exists when virtual machines running under CP are using the processor. While in this state the processor is effectively carrying out work.

TVRATIO

The TVRATIO is used as a measure of the VM overhead. It is calculated as a ratio of TTIME against VTIME. TTIME is the total time taken for an application to process. VTIME is the time that the application code itself was processing, i.e., the time spent in problem state. The difference between TTIME and VTIME is time spent in supervisor state. The TVRATIO cannot be less than one, but the closer the value is to one, the lower the VM overhead.

The figure produced can be used as a guide to the VM overhead, but it should be remembered that some of the work carried out by CP would have to be carried out by a guest system if CP was not running. Also, any improvements in microcode may reduce TTIME and VTIME. This would, in fact, increase the TVRATIO value and make the system appear less efficient.

WAIT STATES

The VM control program can be put into one of three wait states. They are:

• Idle
• Page
• I/O

Idle

This indicates that CP has nothing to do and no work is being processed.

Page

A page wait indicates that at least half (usually more) of the virtual machines are themselves in a page wait state. This makes identification of paging problems much harder. Paging problems can best be identified by looking at page rates and queues on the paging volumes.

I/O

This indicates that the system is waiting, but not in an idle wait or page wait.

Guest Systems

A guest system may be in one of four wait states. These are:

• Page
• I/O
• PSW
• EX

Page A page wait occurs when the guest system is suspended while the control program fetches a page for it. With handshaking (see Chapter 4), page waits are rarely seen. Therefore, a guest system that is doing a lot of paging, typically, cannot be identified from page waits.

I/O An I/O wait occurs when the guest system is suspended while VM starts an I/O for it. As most guests use SIOF (Start I/O Fast), these days an I/O wait is rarely seen.

PSW A PSW wait is sometimes called a voluntary wait. If a guest system has no work to do, it will load a wait PSW. This usually occurs when it is waiting for an I/O operation to complete. If handshaking is used, the guest may be waiting for a page. The problem for systems programmers is that if there are lots of PSW waits, they may be caused by the guest having no work to do or by an I/O problem or a paging problem.

EX An execution wait is also known as a console function wait. This will occur whenever VM simulates an instruction for the guest or whenever VM executes a CP command for it.

ACTIVE WAITS

Since HPO release 3.4, active waits have been available with multiprocessors. Without active wait an inactive processor will load a wait state and spend a lot of time checking with the other processor for work. This will cause the other processor to be interrupted. With active wait the inactive processor will attempt to take work from the queue of the other processor. This will not interrupt the second processor. If it finds no work the first time it will keep on checking.

With XA SP release 1, active wait is required for 3080s, 3090s, and 4381s. One consequence of this is that the System Activity Display (SAD) frame will always show 100 percent busy. To avoid this the SAD frame can be set up so that work that is not supervisor or associated with storage key 3, is separated from the rest and displayed.

Guest systems running in a dedicated processor will not have a SAD display that is 100 percent busy because active wait is not used, however, the Guest Wait State Interpretation Capability (GWSIC) is used.

CONTROL BLOCKS

Each virtual machine has an entry in the directory, but when it is running it is described to CP by control blocks. The VMBLOK describes the virtual machine's attributes, including its running status. With XA the equivalent control block is VMDBK. Other control blocks used include VCHBLOK, which is the virtual channel control block; VCUBLOK, which is the virtual control unit block; VDEVBLOK, which is the virtual device block. With XA these are more or less replaced by the HCPDEV control block.

REAL STORAGE LAYOUT

Real storage is the name given to storage space inside the processor. It is also sometimes called main storage and central storage. Real storage is divided into five areas. These are:

• Nucleus area
• Trace table
• Free Storage Area (FSA)
• Optional guest operating system (V=R)
• Dynamic Paging Area (DPA)

This is illustrated in Figures 2-2, 2-3, and 2-4 showing the set-up for VM/SP, HPO, and XA, respectively. The DPA is the area that can be used by virtual machines for paging into. Only pages in real storage can be processed. Therefore, to maximize the throughput of work done by all virtual machines, it is necessary to ensure that the DPA is as large as possible.

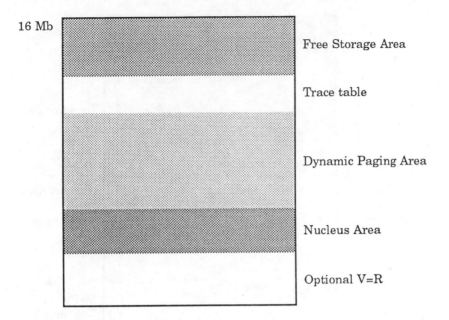

Figure 2-2   SP real storage layout.

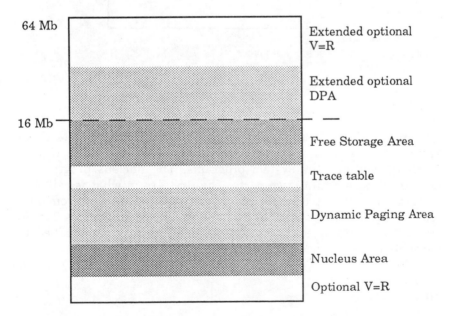

Figure 2-3   HPO real storage layout.

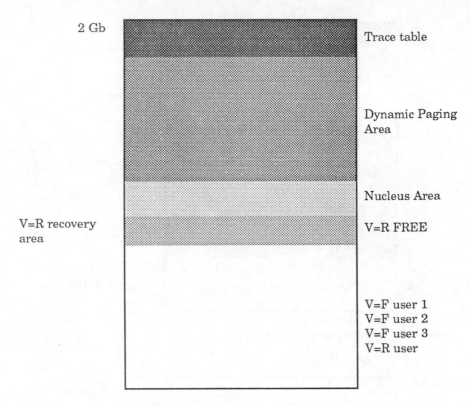

Figure 2-4   XA SP real storage layout.

Nucleus Area

The nucleus is made up of those programs that make the VM CP act like VM rather than any other operating system, e.g., VSE. In other words, it contains the system programs. The nucleus programs, in fact, are separated into two parts. The first are in what is called the resident nucleus. It contains those programs that must remain in real storage at all times. This is the part labeled in Figures 2-2, 2-3, and 2-4 as the nucleus area. The others are in what is called the pageable nucleus, and this actually uses DPA space.

Trace Table

The trace table is used to record events that occur in CP for diagnostic purposes. Data is continuously written into the trace table in a wraparound manner. This means that new data will overwrite old data. The trace table is used by some monitor packages. The data is used to produce reports on system performance.

Free Storage Area

With SP and HPO, part of real storage is allocated to the Free Storage Area (FSA). This area is used by the CP as a working storage area. It is used for various control blocks, e.g., virtual device blocks, spool file blocks, and certain tables, e.g., page and swap tables.

If the system runs out of space in the FSA, it takes space from the DPA. This is always the DPA below the 16 MB line and is called a free storage extend.

With HPO there is a section of free storage allocated as Prime Free Storage. This consists of cache-aligned 128-byte blocks of storage. Prime areas are used by the system for some of its most common and dynamic control blocks, e.g., CPEXBLOK, SAVEAREA, IOBLOK. The default size for the Prime area is 10 percent of the FSA.

With XA, the FSA is not defined, but space is taken from the DPA as required by the FSA.

FSA Contents   A large part of the FSA is taken up by page and swap tables. It is estimated that 3000 bytes per megabyte of virtual storage are required for each logged on user.

Spool file blocks use large amounts of the FSA. 128 bytes are used per spool file. There can frequently be large numbers of spool files on the machine, particularly with PROFS systems installed. However, with VM release 5 and above, spool file control blocks are kept in a separate address space.

Each logged on virtual machine will have a minimum of 6K of the FSA allocated to it. This value could be increased depending on the configuration of the virtual machine.

To give an example of the typical set-up for a virtual machine that has 1M of storage allocated in its directory entry, we note that this virtual machine would require:

- Virtual storage
  - segment tables   64 bytes per MB
  - page tables   768 bytes per MB
  - swap tables   2176 bytes per MB

- Virtual devices
VDEVBLOK	720 bytes
VCTLUNIT	200 bytes
VCHANNEL	192 bytes
- Miscellaneous
Retrieve buffer	160 bytes
PFK table	192 bytes
SSBLOK	320 bytes
SFBLOK	1280 bytes

This gives a minimum of 6072 bytes per user. A sophisticated user with, for example, 8 MB of storage, 30 virtual devices, and 50 spool files would require 34,000 bytes.

Optional Guest Operating System (V=R)

If a guest operating system is run V=R (i.e., virtual = real), it will occupy some of the real storage space available. Typically the guest system run in this way will be MVS. With XA one V=R guest can be run and up to five V=F guests (i.e., virtual = fixed).

V=R FREE Area With XA, the V=R FREE area is the guest operating system recovery area, and its size depends on its usage. It is usually set at between 60 and 80 pages for each V=R and V=F user rather than the 1 MB default. The size of the V=R FREE area is specified by the VRFREE parameter of the SYSSTORE macro in HCPSYS. It must be big enough to recover V=R and V=F areas automatically in the event of an abend. The actual space required can be automatically increased, and a message is displayed on the console.

Dynamic Paging Area

The Dynamic Paging Area (DPA) is the area of real storage that contains page frames made up of the working sets of virtual machines. Only when a virtual machine has a page in the DPA can the instructions in that page be processed. The larger the space available for the DPA, the less paging and swapping required and, therefore, the better overall improved performance that will be achieved. The contents of the page frames in the DPA will change during the life of the system as pages from different virtual machines are brought in and out. In addition to page frames, the DPA may contain the pageable nucleus and DisContiguous Saved Segments (DCSSs). With HPO, VMBLOKs are allocated in the DPA.

One advantage with HPO is that the DPA area can be split above and below the 16 MB line. However, if a required page resides above the line, it must first be migrated to below the line before it can be used. The size of the extended DPA is specified by the RMSIZE parameter of the SYSCOR macro in DMKSYS system module.

SYSTEM MODULES

With SP and HPO there are three important system modules incorporated within the CP nucleus which are used to define the VM environment. They are:

- DMKRIO
- DMKSNT
- DMKSYS

With XA the most important system module is HCPSYS, which is similar in function to DMKSYS.

DMKRIO

The DMKRIO module is used to identify all the real I/O devices that the CP will be aware of, and their configuration. The DMKRIO macros include RDEVICE macros, RCTLUNIT macros, and RCHANNEL macros. Each entry in DMKRIO is used to build control blocks that are stored in main storage. These control blocks contain such information as device type and device address. If a new device is installed, it cannot be used by VM until it is defined in DMKRIO. With XA, new devices need to be specified in the Input Output Configuration DataSet (IOCDS), which is resident on the processor controller unit (3082 or 3092).

DMKSNT

The DMKSNT module contains the system name table which is used to identify the names and locations of core-image code segments. DMKSNT contains resource definitions, including the virtual memory location selected for execution, the CP DASD, space allocation for the saved software, and a specification of how much of the software is shared among users. Any changes to DMKSNT typically require a SYSGEN and IPL.

It also contains network control programs, 3800 printer data arrays, and national language repositories. The macros it contains include NAMESYS, NAMENCP, NAME3800, and NAMELANG.

Saved System Saved systems were introduced in the early 1970s as a way of improving system efficiency. A saved system is a virtual operating system that is IPLable by name instead of device address. It can be shared among many users and thereby reduces the need for users to have their own copy and, therefore, saves space in the DPA. An example is CMS.

Discontiguous Saved Segments Discontiguous saved segments (DCSSs) are similar to saved systems in that most can be shared by many users (provided that the code is reentrant), again saving on DPA space. They contain software that is loaded by CP function rather than by virtual I/O. An area of virtual memory must be allocated for each one to process in, and it is necessary to ensure that the spaces allocated for DCSSs do not overlap.

DMKSYS

The DMKSYS module contains macros that specify parameters which determine system performance, i.e., system definitions. Some of the more common macros are:

- SYSCOR
- SYSJRL
- SYSMON
- SYSOPR
- SYSOWN
- SYSPAG
- SYSRES

SYSCOR The SYSCOR macro specifies the maximum main storage size, e.g., for SP:

```
SYSCOR RMSIZE=16M
```

SYSJRL The SYSJRL macro specifies journaling options which record resource usage. For example, CP accounting records can be produced for unsuccessful access attempts by using the JOURNAL =
YES option.

SYSMON The SYSMON macro specifies the parameters that are to
be used in the collection of performance monitoring data. The data
collected is subsequently sent to a virtual reader.

SYSOPR The SYSOPR macro specifies the system operator user-id
and the user-id that will get the system dump after a system restart.

SYSOWN The SYSOWN macro specifies the disk packs that are to
be used by CP for TEMP, PERM, DRCT, and TDSK areas.
  For SP, an example of the macro would be:

```
SYSOWN (SYSRES,TEMP),(SYSPAG,PAGE)
```

SYSPAG With HPO, the SYSPAG macro is used to specify the
SWAP and PAGE areas on disk, etc. It is recommended that the
SYSPAG macro is never duplicated when adding extra PAGE or
SWAP areas. If it is duplicated, the additional devices specified will
only be used when all devices listed in the first macro are full up.
Therefore, new devices should be added to the existing macro. Also,
when four or more packs are specified, they should be balanced by
placing them on different channels.

SYSRES The SYSRES macro specifies on which DASD and where
on the DASD the major system areas are to be located. These are
shown in Figure 2-5. An example of the way they are defined is
given below:

```
SYSRES  SYSVOL=CPDSK1,                          X
        SYSRES=230,                             X
        SYSTYPE=3380,                           X
        SYSNUC=1,                               X
        SYSERR=3,                               X
        SYSWRM=5
```

  The CP FORMAT and ALLOCATE (DMKFMT) commands are
used to specify the DRCT, PERM, and TDSK areas, e.g.:

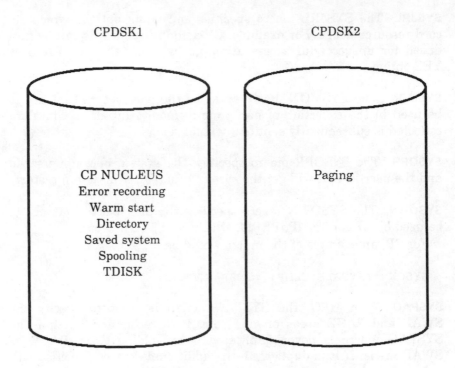

Figure 2-5   System areas on disk.

```
FORMAT,150,3380,CPDSK1,000,007
ALLOCATE,150,3380,CPDSK1
DRCT,001,002
PERM,003,083
TDSK,084,403
END
```

This is shown in Figure 2-6. Many sites place the SYSWRM (warm start), SYSCKP (checkpoint start), and SYSERR (error recording) files on the spool pack as a way of improving performance.

CP-OWNED DASD AREAS

CP-owned DASD contains four areas that are required for the system to function. These are:

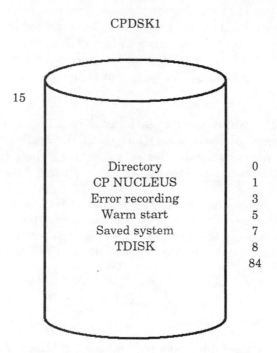

Figure 2-6   Formatted system disk.

- PERM
- TEMP
- TDSK
- DRCT

PERM

The PERM area is divided into a number of areas. It contains CP nucleus, error recording, warm start, and saved system areas.

CP Nucleus The CP nucleus part of the PERM area contains the code that will be loaded in at IPL time. These are the basic system programs or modules. In addition, the CP transient nodules are included here.

Error Recording   The error recording area contains information about errors that occur on devices. The errors are classified as I/O errors or machine check errors. The stored data can be processed using the CPEREP command. This will produce reports and may optionally clear data from the area. The program is usually run on a regular basis.

Warm Start   The warm start area is used to allow a warm start of VM. It contains all the information about the state of the system, including pointers to spool files, etc., so that when the system is started it will continue processing as though it had never stopped.

Saved System Areas   As mentioned earlier, the saved system areas contain codes that can be shared among a number of users. It is quicker to load once, being stored like this, than each user having to load from disk every time they need to use it. CMS is an example of a saved system.

TEMP

TEMP space is used for spooling and paging space. Any space not allocated is assumed to be TEMP.

TDSK

The TDSK area contains temporary mini-disks. These act as a scratchpad area and can be allocated by any virtual machine user. They are deallocated when a user logs off or uses the CP command to deallocate them.

DRCT

The DRCT area contains the system directory.

DIRECTORY

The system directory contains an entry for every virtual machine that can log-on to VM. There are, in fact, two versions—one that is the current in-use directory and one that is a back-up. When a new directory is being implemented, directory blocks are written to the back-up version. Only when the entire directory has been written is the pointer to the directory updated to point to the new area. It is located on the DRCT area of one of the CP-owned DASD.

Contents

The directory entries are stored one after the other, making it a long sequential file. A sample directory entry for a user is given below:

```
USER TREVOR LPWORD 1M 2M ACEG
ACCOUNT NUMBER 123456E
OPTION REALTIMER ECMODE
CONSOLE 009 3215 A
SPOOL 00C 2540 READER A
SPOOL 00D 2540 PUNCH A
SPOOL 00E 1403 A
LINK MAINT 191 291 RR
LINK CMSSYS 190 290 RR
LINK DOSVSE 240 240 RR
MDISK 151 3380 050 060 VMDSK4 MR RPWORD WPWORD
MWPWORD
MDISK 152 3380 061 070 VMDSK4 MR RPWORD WPWORD
MWPWORD
```

This identifies the user by user-id and specifies the password to be entered at log-on time. It also specifies the primary and secondary real storage allocation that the virtual machine will appear to receive. This is the user's virtual address space. The letters following this specify the command classes that can be used. The other entries specify the virtual machine configuration by giving the virtual console, the virtual reader, and virtual punch. The mini-disks associated with the virtual machine are specified as are any other user's mini-disks that it can use.

Directory Maintenance

The directory file can be updated using the CMS command DIRECT. However, this is usually not the best way because at most sites the file is so large as to make this cumbersome. The use of a package to help with directory maintenance is the norm and the package most frequently used is DIRMAINT.

The directory maintenance package requires two virtual machines. One is called DIRMAINT and is the directory manager. The other is called DATAMOVE and performs copying and formatting tasks.

Before a new entry can be made it is important to perform a diskmap. The diskmap will show where there is space on a disk for the new mini-disks to be defined. It will also show areas of overlap of mini-disks. Apart from MAINT and the machine for DDR back-up, there should not be any overlap. It can lead to security and data integrity problems if users' mini-disks do overlap.

OTHER VM FEATURES

There are certain aspects of the VM environment that exist at every site, but have not been discussed before. These include the use of PROFILE EXEC, AUTOLOG, and the MAINT user-id.

PROFILE EXEC

Whenever CMS is IPLed, either automatically from the directory entry or explicitly by the user, it executes a file called PROFILE EXEC as part of its initialization process. The PROFILE EXEC can be used to tailor the user's environment to suit the particular requirements of that user. Entries might include:

* Specifying SET commands
* Accessing any libraries that will be required for programming
* Accessing any additional disks not specified in the directory
* Establishing distribution and routing information for a virtual printer
* Setting PF key definitions

An example of a PROFILE EXEC is given below.

```
'CP SPOOL CONSOLE  DIST ABC100'
'CP SPOOL PRINTER ROUTE ABC123 DIST ABC100'
'CP SPOOL PUNCH DIST ABC123'
GLOBAL MACLIB CMSLIB
GLOBAL TXTLIB PLILIB
```

Similar to a PROFILE EXEC is a PROFILE XEDIT file. This file will tailor the XEDIT environment to whatever a user requires. The file is executed whenever XEDIT is invoked.

AUTOLOG

At system start-up time it is usual to start a disconnected system called AUTOLOG. This typically contains the start-up commands for a number of systems to save the operator having to remember to key them in in the correct sequence. It can also contain various SET commands to define the VM environment for that session.

MAINT

MAINT is a user-id that is used by systems programmers to maintain the system. The S and Y disks belong to MAINT and these are linked to by all other CMS users. The MAINT user-id is usually set up so that it can issue all the CP and CMS commands; i.e., there are no restrictions.

PROCESSING SUMMARY

When a user logs-on to the system, he will be allocated the amount of space in virtual storage that is specified in the directory entry for that user. The space is formatted into 4K pages, and it is these pages that contain the program code and data that the virtual machine uses.

In order to process, pages must be copied into real storage inside the processor. However, because VM allows multitasking, there will be pages from many other virtual machines also in real storage competing for the use of the processor. In order that CP can make a selection, each virtual machine is allocated a priority value and assigned to a queue. A component of the System Resource Manager (SRM) called the scheduler is responsible for this. There are three queues, one for each of three categories of work. Queue 1 is typically made up of interactive CMS users. Queue 2 usually contains users performing a long computation that does not require any I/O from the terminal; and queue 3 contains guest operating systems.

When a virtual machine is at the front of its queue it will be processed by a component called the dispatcher. Each type of work is allocated a limited amount of time. If the task does not complete within that time limit, the job may be moved into a different queue (e.g., queue 1 to queue 2). At the end of its time limit a new priority for the task is calculated and it will be put back on one of the queues.

While a virtual machine is processing, pages may be brought in from virtual storage containing either data or instructions. When the timeslice has completed, pages may be copied out to auxiliary storage and the space in real storage made available for other virtual machines to use.

When a user logs off, the space in virtual storage that it was using is made available for other users.

This process is examined in more detail in Chapters 3 and 4. The above summary is given to provide the reader with an overview of how VM works and what is happening while work is being processed.

3

Processing

The management of VM performance requires some understanding of how logged on virtual machines are processed. This chapter sets out to describe how processing works; it details the various components involved and looks at the algorithm used by the software components in selecting work for processing.

All virtual machines that are logged on to the system fall under the control of either the scheduler or the dispatcher. The scheduler looks after idle users and eligible users. An eligible user is one who would like to be active; i.e., the user has entered something at the keyboard, but is not yet active. The dispatcher looks after those virtual machines that are active. A user will move from the eligible queue to the dispatchable queue when there is room for his pages to move into the Dynamic Paging Area (DPA) of real storage. The order in which virtual machines are dispatched depends on their dispatching priority.

SCHEDULER

When a virtual machine has some work to process, it wants to be dispatched. The scheduler's job is to organize the competing virtual machines to make the dispatcher's job as straightforward as possible. To do this the scheduler maintains two lists. The first list contains those virtual machines that are eligible for dispatching but cannot

31

start because their working set requirements (i.e., the number of real storage page frames that they require) are in excess of the number of currently available page frames. This list is called the eligible list. The second list contains those virtual machines whose working sets are in real storage and could be selected for processing by the dispatcher. This list is sometimes known as the runnable list, but a more suitable name might be the dispatchable list.

A virtual machine that is waiting to execute will be placed in one of three queues. These queues are known as Q1, Q2, and Q3. The user is, therefore, called an in-queue user. Movement between queues is controlled by the scheduler. There are separate lists for each of the three queues. When a user changes from one queue to another, he is placed on the eligible list for that queue rather than the dispatchable queue.

The scheduler will calculate the working set requirements and the deadline priority for all in-queue users. The method for calculating the deadline priority is described later.

The function of the scheduler is, therefore, to maximize system throughput and to maintain user response times. This it achieves by the discretionary allocation of CPU resources.

Q1

A virtual machine in queue 1 is given the shortest time interval or timeslice. For example, a virtual machine executing in Q1 might be allocated 5 milliseconds to complete all instructions before being interrupted. The time allocation for all queues is dependent on the processor hardware. Queue 1 will contain interactive users that do not utilize the processor for long periods of time. Typically these will be CMS users. The size of queue 1 is dependent on the multiprogramming level.

Q2

A virtual machine in queue 2 is given the second shortest time interval. For example, a virtual machine executing in Q2 might be allocated 40 milliseconds. This queue will typically contain noninteractive users that use considerable amounts of processor time but are rarely interrupted for slow speed I/O operations.

Q3

A virtual machine in queue 3 is given the longest time interval. For example, a virtual machine executing in Q3 might be allocated 320 milliseconds. This queue will contain virtual machines that require very large amounts of processor time. They will almost certainly be guest operating systems such as VSE or MVS.

QUEUING SEQUENCE

All virtual machines will start out in eligible Q1. They will then be scheduled for dispatching, and be put in dispatchable Q1. The fair share dispatcher will select them for processing. If at the end of the timeslice allocated to the machine it has not completed all its instructions, the machine will be moved to eligible Q2; otherwise it will stay in Q1.

The scheduler will move the virtual machine from eligible Q2 to dispatchable Q2 when there are enough page frames available for its working set requirements to be met. When the user has the highest priority of any job in the queue, it will be dispatched. A virtual machine in Q2 that executes for between five and eight (depending on the processor) consecutive timeslices without becoming idle before the end of the allotted timeslice will be placed in eligible Q3. Otherwise it will stay in Q2.

A virtual machine in eligible Q3 will pass to the dispatchable Q3 only when all the usual requirements can be met. It will then sit in dispatchable Q3 until it is selected for processing.

There is no Q4.

DISPATCHER

The dispatcher is known as a fair share dispatcher. When it dispatches virtual machines, it takes no account of any internal activity such as can occur within a guest operating system.

The dispatcher will select a Q2 user eight times less often than a Q1 user. It will select a Q3 user 64 times less often than a Q1 user. However, they are allocated longer timeslices in which to process. The currently active virtual machine is called the runuser.

A virtual machine that is dispatched will continue processing instructions until one of the following events occur:

- It reaches the end of its timeslice.
- A privileged operation requires CP simulation.
- A real machine interrupt occurs (e.g., an I/O interrupt).

PRIORITY

At the end of each user's timeslice the priority for his next dispatch (i.e., his deadline priority) is calculated by the scheduler based on the user's activity in relation to other active users on the system. He is placed in the queue in the position that is appropriate to his priority value.

DEADLINE PRIORITY

The priority value assigned to a user within a queue is called the deadline priority, and it is recalculated at each queue drop. Queue drop is the name given to what happens at the end of each virtual machine's timeslice. Deadline priority is based on a number of parameters. These are listed below:

- The user priority as specified in the directory entry for that user or as modified using the SET PRIORITY user-id nn command. The value will be in the range of 1 to 99 with a default value of 64. The lower the number, the better the priority.
- The nature of the work to be done.
- The current system paging load—this will affect the average response times.
- The user's contribution to this load (i.e., his relative main storage requirement).
- The amount of main storage contention.

By using a deadline priority system, the dispatcher ensures that no single virtual machine with a high priority value in its directory monopolizes the processor resources and impairs the performance of the other virtual machines.

DEADLINE PRIORITY CALCULATION

The deadline priority specifies a time by which the virtual machine is expected to have used its next timeslice. The calculation takes

Table 3-1   Relationship between queue and F1 value.

Queue	F1
1	1/8
2	1
3	8

place after each queue drop. The method of calculation for SP and HPO is as follows:

Deadline priority = time of day + delay factor

The delay factor is calculated as follows:

Delay factor = urgency coefficient + average response time

The urgency coefficient is calculated as follows:

Urgency coefficient = $F1 + F2 + F3$

where $F1$ is a function depending on Q; $F2$ is a measure of resource utilization by the virtual machine whose deadline priority is being calculated; and $F3$ is a function of the user priority specified in the directory.

The urgency coefficient for an average user is one.

The $F1$ value can be obtained from the values shown in Table 3-1.

$F2$ is determined by measuring resource utilization. It is calculated as follows:

$F2$ = CPU ratio * (100 − page bias) + working set ratio * page bias

The CPU ratio is calculated as follows:

CPU ratio = $CPU time used/_{average CPU time used}$

This value should be one.

The working set ratio is calculated as follows:

$$Working\ set\ ratio = {}^{user's\ working\ set\ size}\!/\!_{average\ working\ set\ size}$$

The scheduler will also calculate a page bias function. This gives an indication of how long the user has spent in the eligible list, i.e., waiting for storage.

The page bias is calculated as follows:

$$Page\ bias = k * {}^{a}\!/\!_{a+q}$$

where a is the average eligible list time and q is the in-queue time. k is a variable whose value depends on the processor type used.

$F3$ is calculated as follows:

$$F3 = {}^{priority\ value\ in\ directory}\!/\!_{64}$$

Alternative Calculation

An alternative simplified way to calculate deadline priority is to use the formula:

$$Deadline\ priority = time\ of\ day + (timeslice * number\ of\ users)$$

The calculation is further complicated by:

$$Deadline\ priority =$$

$$time\ of\ day + (timeslice * number\ of\ users) * userpriority * {}^{amount\ already\ used}\!/\!_{fair\ share}$$

Assuming that there are 10 active users on the system, the CPU is 100 percent busy, and a timeslice is 0.1 seconds, a user can expect to take 1 second to get his 0.1 second timeslice. The deadline time for that user would be calculated as time of day plus 1 second. This value would be modified by usage history. Therefore, if the user has been getting less than his fair share, his deadline value will be reduced. If he has been getting more than his fair share, his deadline value will be increased. A reduction in deadline priority will result in improved response time.

Typically, the usage variables are smoothed exponentially over an 8-minute period. The effect of this is that a user who becomes active after a period of inactivity will get better than average service for the first few minutes. Eventually the scheduler will restore the service level for that user to normal. In fact, a user who starts a highly compute-bound job after being idle on a system with very few users on it will get far more than his fair share for several minutes. This will, consequently, degrade the performance of existing users.

In theory, the fair share calculations are based on the weighted average of a virtual machine's usage of CPU cycles and storage. The initial setting is to weight CPU at 100 percent and storage at 0 percent. If paging is very light, this value might never change. Typically, the weight used in calculations is varied by the feedback module according to the current system performance.

SWAPPED OUT USERS

With HPO, when a swapped out user is added to one of the three queues, a number of swap sets is swapped in immmediately. This number is specified by the SET SRM PREPAGE command, and the value may be different for Q1 and Q2 users. The value should not be higher than the number of channels used for swapping so that all swap sets can be read at the same time. For Q2 users a value of one is usually sufficient.

4

Paging

Any given piece of work will usually perform the same number of I/O operations and use the same amount of CPU resources each time it is run. However, the amount of paging that takes place will depend on the mix of work running on the system at the time and also on the tuning parameters that are in effect. This chapter examines paging and performance. It overviews some of the basic terminology; looks at real storage layout including the Dynamic Paging Area; examines the whole paging process; discusses paging with a guest operating system; and finally explores I/O and auxiliary storage considerations.

VIRTUAL STORAGE CONCEPTS

Most of the early processors had a comparatively small amount of core available to run programs in. This led to the development of virtual storage. *Virtual storage* is storage space within the processor that appears to be available. So, for example, a processor with only 256K of internal storage could process a program that was 1 MB in size. The days of ferrite core storage are long past, and the names now given to this internal storage are *real storage*, *main storage*, and *central storage*. The additional space required to store the program is called *auxiliary storage*. Auxiliary storage typically exists on disks but may exist on special paging devices or within expanded storage.

Virtual storage is, therefore, made up of real storage and auxiliary storage.

Real storage is divided into a number of areas including the Dynamic Paging Area (DPA). The DPA can contain pages from active virtual machines. With SP the maximum size of real storage that can be supported is 16 MB. With HPO, the maximum size of real storage space is 64 MB. With XA, the maximum real storage size rises to 2 GB.

When a virtual machine logs-on, it will be allocated an amount of virtual storage space dependent on the value specified in the directory entry for that virtual machine. This space will be formatted into 4K blocks called pages. The pages are all placed on auxiliary storage, and some of them are copied into real storage. Only pages in real storage can have the instructions within them processed. Auxiliary storage is formatted into 4K units called *page slots*. Real storage is formatted into 4K units called *page frames*. This is illustrated in Figure 4-1.

The page frames that are allocated to a virtual machine within real storage, or the page frames that it requires, are called its *working set*. The movement of a page from auxiliary storage to real storage is called a *page-in*. The movement of a page from real storage to auxiliary storage is called a *page-out*.

The ability of the processor to have more than one virtual machine logged on at any one time is called multiprogramming. The processor can be carrying out the instructions from one virtual machine, while another is waiting for an I/O activity to complete, and a third is waiting for a user to complete a typing activity and press the enter key. If lots of users are logged on, those that have instructions that the processor could carry out are kept in a queue and dealt with as quickly as possible (see Chapter 3). Some processor complexes have more than one processor and so can carry out two (or more, depending on configuration) instructions at the same time. This process is called multiprocessing.

If the next instruction to be processed, for an active virtual machine, exists in a page that is not in real storage, a *page fault* occurs. The virtual machine cannot continue processing until the page that is required has been paged in; therefore, it will be interrupted and another virtual machine will become active. The page-in operation is known as *demand paging*. A copy of the required page is copied from auxiliary storage into a page frame in real storage.

If there are currently no free page frames available for a page-in activity, CP will take an unreferenced page from another user. This is called *page stealing*. Sometimes CP will steal pages from one user

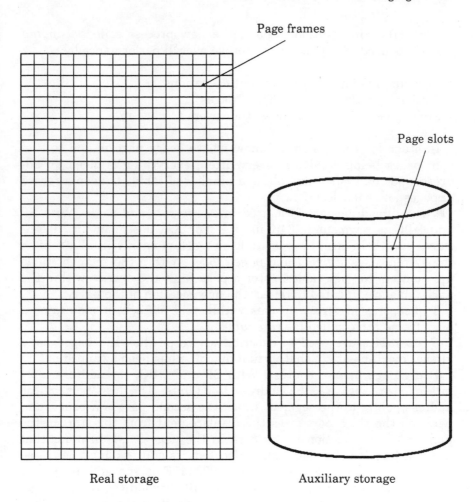

Figure 4-1   Virtual storage.

to satisfy the working set requirements of another user only to find that almost immediately it needs to page-in the contents of the pages that it had deallocated. To satisfy the working set requirements of the first user, pages will be stolen, possibly from the second user. A problem occurs if page-ins and page stealing become excessive because the processor will be in supervisor state handling paging rather than being in problem state and processing the instructions within the pages. This process is called *thrashing*. One obvious effect is that response times for virtual machines will deteriorate.

With HPO, in addition to paging, a new process called *swapping* was introduced. Swapping can improve overall performance by:

• Reducing I/O for page-in/page-out operations
• Speeding up the bulk transfer of pages
• Freeing page frames to allow other users to page-in

In order for the system to know where every page is and to prevent pages being accidently overwritten, everything is given an address, and the system maintains a number of tables to keep a record of pages and their location.

Virtual machines are formatted into *segments* and pages. With SP and HPO, a segment is 64K in size. For XA, a segment is 1024K. Pages are 4K in size. In order to keep track of each virtual machine, the system uses *segment* and *page tables*. Within the segment table are pointers to page tables. After a page fault the entries within the page table are updated to reflect the new location of the page.

To keep track of page frames within real storage, it maintains a page frame table called the *core table*.

Swap tables are used to describe where on disk the pages for a virtual machine are, if that virtual machine has been swapped out.

Every page has an address. With SP and HPO, the address is 24 bits in size, with XA the address is 31 bits. The first part of the address points to the segment table, the second part is a page number, and the third part gives the displacement from the start of the page of the instruction (i.e., where in the page it is). In order that the real location of a page can be located, its address must be translated. If, for example, an address of 23447E is the address of the next instruction to be processed and it falls beyond the range of real storage addresses, CP will look up segment 23 in the segment table. This will give the address of the appropriate page table. It will look up page 4, which will give a virtual address of 67000. Therefore, the address of the next instruction is 6747E. The address of the next instruction to be processed is also contained in the second part of the program status word (PSW).

REAL STORAGE LAYOUT

As decribed in Chapter 1, real storage is basically divided into four areas. These are:

- Free Storage Area (FSA)
- Trace table
- Nucleus area
- Dynamic Paging Area (DPA)

There may also be an optional guest operating system that is running V=R which will occupy part of real storage.

The DPA is the area that can be used by the pages of virtual machines for processing. More user pages can be contained in the DPA and, therefore, more useful work performed if the DPA is maintained at the maximum size possible.

With SP the maximum size for real storage is 16 MB, as this is the maximum size that can be addressed using 24 bit addressing. With HPO the maximum size for real storage is 64 MB. This is possible because real storage management uses 26 bit addressing. With XA the maximum size is 2 GB, which is the maximum size possible using 31 bit addressing.

Free Storage Area

With SP and HPO the Free Storage Area (FSA) is used for various control blocks including virtual device blocks, spool file blocks, and certain tables, e.g., page and swap tables.

If there is not enough room in the FSA the system takes space from the DPA. This is always the DPA below the 16-MB line. The process is known as a free storage extend, and the occurrences of these should be monitored.

Reducing FSA Usage   To prevent the FSA extending into the DPA space, and also to minimize the size of the FSA, it can be useful to keep to a minimum the contents of the FSA.

With HPO releases above 4.2, unused page and swap tables are automatically migrated to paging devices. For sites using earlier releases, the MIGRATE command can be used, and this will have the same effect.

Reducing the number of spool file blocks can be easily achieved by purging files. User training can be a great help in this respect if users are taught to read in the files that are in their reader queues and then save them to mini-disk. Also many sites write short routines that will delete any spool file that is older than eight days. Sites using PROFS with VM releases lower than 5 often find spool file blocks a real problem. With release 5 and above spool file blocks are kept in virtual storage in a separate address space. This helps to reduce free storage utilization.

Idle users should log off. This will free the 6K or more of FSA they have allocated. This can be accomplished either by training users in the importance of logging off when not performing work involving the processor, or running a program that will FORCE off users who have been idle for a predetermined period of time, e.g., 5 minutes. It must be long enough to allow plenty of thinking time and not annoy or frustrate "slow" users. A PROFS user who logs on in the morning and does not use the system after 9:30 (or log off) will still be using 6K of storage and may be an ideal candidate for forcing off, as a way of reducing the amount of FSA space used.

FSA Size If the FSA allocated is larger than is required, this is wasteful because it takes away space that could be used by the DPA. If the FSA is too small to meet its requirements, it will go through what is known as a free storage extend. In this process it takes away space from the DPA below the 16-MB line. This free storage extend may cause page-out activities for pages that are in the DPA.

The size of the FSA is specified in DMKSYS at IPL time. This is specified as FREE = nn,PRIME = nn. To find out if the value has been correctly specified it is necessary to display the two full words at DMKFRENP in real storage, at regular intervals throughout a working day. If the value of the first full word remains at or near zero, it indicates that the allocated free storage space is adequate for current usage. If the value of the first full word is more than 3E, it is usually worth increasing the amount of free storage space. Calculating how many additional pages are needed is done by subtracting the initial value of the second word displayed from the highest recorded value of the second word displayed. This value is in hex and will have to be converted to decimal. The DMKSYS FREE parameter can be increased by the calculated amount. As a general rule, after any change is made to the system, the system should be monitored to ensure that only the desired effect was achieved.

With VM/XA SP there is no free storage area as such specified in the HCPSYS module. Any required space is obtained dynamically from the DPA.

Trace Table

The trace table is used to record events that occur in CP for diagnostic purposes. It is also used by some monitor packages for extracting information about system performance.

The default size for the trace table is set at 4 pages for every 1 MB of real storage up to 16 MB. For real storage above 16 MB the value is 1 page for every 1 MB. This would give, for example, 400K of real storage allocated for trace tables on a machine running HPO with 64 MB of real storage. This value is regarded by many as being unnecessarily high. With XA SP the default size for trace tables is one page for every 64K of real storage.

With HPO release 5 and above, the value for trace tables can be specified by the SYSCOR TRACE= parameter in DMKSYS. The less space that is allocated to trace tables, the more space that can be made available for the DPA. With XA the size of the trace tables is specified by the TRACE option on the SYSSTORE macro of HCPSYS.

It has been suggested that a production system could run with 16K allocated for trace tables. If problems should be experienced on the system, then an alternative nucleus with full-size trace tables should be used for diagnosing the problem. Typically, it is not very practical to IPL a new system and then to try to recreate the problem. Most sites tend to use a trace table size somewhere between 16K and the default value.

Nucleus Area

The nucleus is made up of the CP system programs. It is divided into two parts, a resident nucleus and a pageable nucleus. The resident nucleus will typically occupy about 100 pages and occupies the nucleus area in real storage. The size of this resident nucleus may be reduced by:

• Removing unwanted devices from DMKRIO
• Removing (i.e., deleting from the CP loadlist) those modules that are considered to be unnecessary in the environment where the CP is running

However, the savings in space will usually be small and will not significantly increase the size of the DPA. Also, if an attempt is made to use a removed function CP will abend.

With VM/SP release 5, the following functions can be removed:

- Multiple address space guest
- SNA(CCS)
- TTY terminals
- 3066 device support
- Remote 3270
- 3375 and 3380 device support
- 3704, 3705, 3720, and 3725 controller support
- 3850 support
- 3800 support

The total saving achievable is about 66K.

With HPO release 5, the list is similar to the SP list with the addition of:

- Local 3270
- PMA
- V=R
- V=R recovery
- Quiesce command
- Missing interrupt handler

Not available for removal from the list is 3800 support. The total saving achievable is about 80K.

Performance improvements can be achieved by moving some entries from the pageable to the resident nucleus, for example, the IUCV modules. Although this will increase the size of the nucleus area and, therefore, decrease the space available to the DPA, it may give positive benefits in performance.

Optional (V=R) Area

When a guest operating system is run V=R, it will occupy some of the real storage space available. The larger the area that it occupies, the less space that can be allocated to the DPA. Most often the guest system run in this way will be MVS. The amount of space allocated is usually decided upon in response to the requirements of the guest system and its users. With VM/SP all the space allocated to this guest will come from the bottom of real storage, i.e., page one up-wards. With HPO space can also be allocated at the top end of real storage. It is always good policy to attempt to balance areas above and below the 16-MB line. The space above the line is specified by the RSSIZE parameter of the SYSCOR macro of DMKSYS.

With XA SP the size of the recovery area (V=R FREE) is specified in the HCPSYS SYSSTORE macro VRFREE option. It is necessary for the area to be available in the event of a CP abend to recover guest systems. However, the default size of 1 MB is typically too big. The size required depends on the number of virtual devices in use by the virtual machine and a useful starting value would be 300K per guest system in real storage. If the space is too small, a message will be sent to the VM operator console and appropriate action can be taken. The amount of space to be used can be found by entering LOCATE HCPRSMVE. This will give a real address. The following command is entered D H*address* to show the number of double words in hex currently in use.

Dynamic Paging Area

This, the area of real storage that contains page frames, makes up the working sets of virtual machines. It also contains the pageable nucleus. Only when a virtual machine has a page in the DPA can the instructions in that page be processed. The larger the space that is available for the DPA, the less paging and swapping required. A direct consequence of this is an overall improvement in performance. A map of the contents of the DPA is kept by the core table (described later).

If a particular piece of code is to be used by a number of CMS users, they would each have their own copy of the code which would be paged into real storage for processing. A saved system area can be allocated at the top of the DPA to contain one copy of the code which can be used by all the CMS users. This will avoid duplication and save space in the DPA. It will also improve performance for the CMS users by having the code already loaded when they want to use it. DisContiguous Saved Segments (DCSSs) offer similar advantages in reducing the amount of DPA space required and are used for the same reasons.

The size of the DPA can be increased by installing a larger CPU. For SP users it can be increased by migrating to HPO and removing the 16-MB main storage limitation. For users of both SP and HPO a migration to XA SP offers up to 2 GB of main storage, thus making lots more space available for the DPA.

PAGING SUMMARY

The following is a summary of what happens to the pages of a virtual machine while it is logged on.

When a user logs on, the virtual machine size specified in the directory entry for that user is allocated. These pages will be on auxiliary storage. The pages are kept in page slots.

When the user types in a command and presses the enter key, he will stop being "idle" and will become eligible for processing. At queue add time, the contents of pages on auxiliary storage will be copied into the DPA area of real storage. Page frames will be allocated to these pages, which will make up the working set for that user.

While the user is being dispatched, the processor will perform instructions contained within the pages. If the next instruction to be processed is not currently in real storage, a page fault will occur. Processing for the user's virtual machine will be interrupted while demand paging occurs. The processor will process other virtual machines. Once the appropriate page has been paged in, the virtual machine can be scheduled for processing.

While the instructions are being processed, the contents of some of the pages will change while others remain the same. Some of the pages making up the working set will be referenced, others will not.

A user will process until the end of his allotted timeslice or until all instructions are completed. The virtual machine will then go through the queue drop process. (Processing may also be halted by a privileged instruction requiring CP simulation or by a real machine interrupt occurring.)

When the user has no more instructions to process, the working set page frames could become free for use by other virtual machines. With SP, any changed pages must be paged out to auxiliary storage. Any unchanged pages can be overwritten because a copy already exists on auxiliary storage. This can be inefficient if the user starts working again, as pages will have to be paged in to reestablish a working set for that user. With HPO all referenced pages for a user are grouped into a swap set. This swap set will be put on the interactive swap queue. Later, it may be put on the noninteractive swap queue and then swapped out. The unreferenced pages for the user will be placed on the trim set.

With SP, when the user becomes active again, pages must be copied in from the paging area on auxiliary storage. With HPO, the swap set will be swapped in. This is likely to contain the pages that are going to be required by that virtual machine.

When a virtual machine logs off, its page slots on auxiliary storage become free for use by other virtual machines.

To ensure that there are page frames which can be used for page-in and swap-in operations, a list is kept in the freelist (part of the core table). To ensure that enough page frames are listed in the freelist the system maintains a flushlist (also part of the core table). With HPO, a five-stage process using the DMKSEL macro ensures that enough page frames are included in the flushlist to keep up the level required for the freelist.

The number of page-ins that are required can be reduced if a page that is to be used is still in real storage. It can be reclaimed by updating the tables and can then be used.

If there are a large number of users who want to use the CPU at any one time, CP will spend a lot of time paging in and out. This will reduce response times and is called thrashing. Usually when this happens it indicates that more DPA space is required.

THE CORE TABLE

The core table is specified in DMKSYS. Real storage is mapped by the core table, i.e., the core table acts as a page frame table. There is one entry for each page frame. This entry contains details of the status of that frame (i.e., what it is used for and who owns it). Within the core table are two or three lists made of linked pointers. This is illustrated in Figure 4-2. For SP the tables are:

- The freelist
- The flushlist

With HPO there is a third list called:

- The swap queue

With HPO, when a virtual machine is dropped from the queue, the queue drop routine will see if pages have been referenced since the user was last queued. If not, the pages are put on the flushlist. If the answer is yes, the pages are put in the swap queue.

Core table

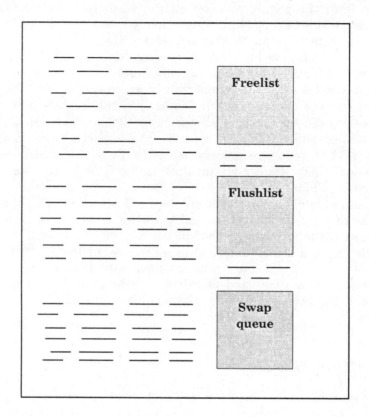

Figure 4-2   The core table and contents.

THE FREELIST

The freelist contains references to all real storage page frames that
are available for use. After an IPL almost all the pages in the DPA
have an entry in the freelist. During the day pages can be added
when a user logs off or when a user performs a reset function, e.g.,
SYSTEM CLEAR.

All page frames that are to be used for page-in operations or for
free storage extends must have an entry in the freelist. Enough page
frames must be kept on the freelist to satisfy any requests.

With SP the number of page frames kept in the freelist is equal to
the number of in-queue users plus one. This is to allow every user to
suffer a page fault and for there to be a free storage extend.

With HPO the number is calculated in the same way, but added to that number is the value of MINNUMSS (see later) multiplied by the swap set size.

MINNUMSS

The MINNUMSS value is the value specified by the SET SRM MINNUMSS command. It is the number of swap sets that will be swapped in. The value used should be high enough to allow for concurrent I/O from all swap devices. By monitoring the availability of frames in the freelist, appropriate values can be set.

Swap Set Size

The swap set size is the number of pages that will be read in together if a page fault occurs for a swapped out page.

THE FLUSHLIST

The flushlist records those real storage page frames that are allocated to users who are not ready to use the CPU. These are pages that are candidates for the freelist.

SWAP QUEUES

Swap queues exist only with HPO. There are separate logical swap queues for interactive and noninteractive users. They contain swap sets (see later) created at queue drop time.

MAINTAINING FREELIST PAGES

When a page fault occurs, the next page that is required will be paged in. It will be placed in an available page frame. The list of available page frames is contained in the freelist. If there are not enough page frames listed in the freelist, CP must take steps to add page frames to this list. With HPO the DMKSEL (select) routine goes through a five-stage process in order to replenish the freelist.

DMKSEL Routine

This is a five-stage process that is used to place in the freelist pointers to page frames that can be used by user pages.

Stage 1 The first stage occurs at four-second intervals. In this, a garbage collector routine searches one-eighth of the DPA looking for any miscellaneous page frames that can be added to the freelist. Miscellaneous pages would include:

- Spool buffer pages
- Transient system address space pages (unreferenced)
- Virtual machine pseudo segments
- Pages belonging to out-of-queue users referenced by CP

Stage 2 Stage 2 involves the movement of users from the interactive to the noninteractive swap queue and to physically swap out pages from the noninteractive queue.

With HPO releases below 5, the length of time that a user spends on each queue can be specified using the SET SRM SWPQTIME command. The default value for the interactive queue is 20 seconds. It should be very slightly more than the time a user spends "thinking" so that the user is not swapped out between interactions. Many sites use the default values. The default value for the noninteractive queue is 100 seconds. Most sites will reduce this value in order to encourage swapping rather than paging. A typical value would be five seconds, although it may be reduced even further if demand paging rates are high. The swap queue time values can be displayed using the QUERY SRM SWPQTIME command.

The actual time spent on queues will be longer than the values specified if there is no contention for storage space.

At this stage, not all the pages in a user's working set will be swapped out. Only enough pages to replenish the freelist will be taken.

Stage 3 With HPO this stage involves pages being taken from the flushlist that had been put there by the garbage collector routine and by trimming (described later). The pages are placed on the freelist. If the contents of any of the pages have changed since they were paged in, the page must be paged out first. Users in Q1 are slightly more favored than users in Q2.

With VM/SP, when replenishing the freelist, CP will attempt to take pages from the flushlist. This is usually empty because flushing only occurs when CP considers that a paging emergency has occurred. If this does occur, all the pages belonging to a user are put on the flushlist when that user is next dropped from the queue. This is bad for performance because the virtual machine will experience page faults when it is next scheduled.

Stage 4 If there are still not enough pages in the freelist, then users will be swapped out even if their swap queue time has not expired. It does this in two steps. In step one it will swap out noninteractive users. In step two it will swap out interactive users. Virtual machines are swapped one at a time in the order first-in, first-out (FIFO).

   If stage four is reached, the system is experiencing storage problems. Use of the QUERY SRM SWPQTIME command will gain more information from the system.

Stage 5 This is the method used by SP because it does not have the ability to swap pages. With HPO it is used as a last resort. In this stage the core table is scanned and the reference bit for each page frame is tested. If the reference bit is off, the frame is added to the freelist. If there are no unreferenced pages, CP chooses pages that are unchanged. An unchanged page is one that has been paged in from auxiliary storage, but during the time it has occupied a page frame there has not been any alteration to its contents; i.e., any data has not been updated. During this first pass the reference bits are reset to zero.

   If there are still insufficient page frames for the freelist, the list is scanned again. If there are any pages belonging to in-core users that have not been referenced between the two passes, those pages will be stolen. If the contents of the page to be stolen have been changed, a copy of the contents must first be written out to auxiliary storage (i.e., a page-out operation). If a page has been referenced during the period between the two scanning operations, the reference bit will have changed from zero to 1. When enough page frames have been found, a pointer is kept. When a core table scan next takes place, it will start from that point. This process does tend to favor in-queue users.

   With HPO page steal rates should be monitored and where possible page stealing should be eliminated.

   With SP the time taken for one complete pass of the core table is a good performance indicator. The time indicates how long a page can remain in storage without being referenced. On average out-of-queue users will remain in storage for half of the scan time; i.e., they will be picked by the scan's first pass. The average time for in-queue users is one and a half times the core scan time; i.e., they will be picked up on the scan's second pass.

With SP the optimum scan time should be large enough for the majority of an interactive user's pages to be still in storage when that user rejoins the queue. The scan time must be longer than the user's "think" time. Typically, a scan time value that is acceptable is around 10 seconds.

QUEUE DROP

With HPO, at queue drop time, the pages making up the working set of a virtual machine that have been referenced are grouped into swap sets. The projected new working set size for the user is calculated by the scheduler.

Swap Sets

A swap set will contain the working set pages of a user after that user is dropped from the queue. If the number is below the minimum working set size, unreferenced pages are added to make up the shortfall. This number is specified by the SET MINWS command (see Chapter 6). The swap set is placed on a swap queue and the page table entries are invalidated.

Expanded storage is usually best used for swapping when the swap set size will divide into 128 exactly, i.e., without leaving a remainder.

Trim Set

After the swap set is placed on the swap queue any remaining unreferenced pages for that virtual machine are called the trim set. The entries for the trim set are placed on the flushlist. This process is called *trimming*.

SWAPPED OUT USERS

With HPO, when a swapped out user is added to one of the three queues, a number of swap sets are swapped in immmediately. This number is specified by the SET SRM PREPAGE command and the value may be different for queue 1 and queue 2 users. High values may result in real storage becoming overcommitted. It may, therefore, be necessary to increase the MINNUMSS (minimum number of swap sets) value using the SET SRM MINNUMSS command. The SRM PREPAGE value should be equal to or less than the number of channels used for swapping so that all swap sets can be read at the same time. For queue 2 users a value of one is usually sufficient (SET commands are discussed in more detail in Chapter 6).

XA PAGING

VM/XA does not swap pages in the same way as HPO, but performs something similar known as block paging. In order that locality of reference of pages is preserved on disk, all pages, even if they are unchanged, are written to disk. The effect of this is that higher paging rates are observable.

XA also makes use of seldom ending channel programs (more properly called suspend/resume channel programs). Because of this it is preferable to use dedicated disks for paging. If this is not possible, paging areas should be put on disks with data that are relatively inactive. Pages are allocated to paging devices depending on service times for that device. This means that XA is more likely to page to fast devices than slower devices.

GUEST OPERATING SYSTEMS

It is estimated that about 90 percent of sites with VM installed are running with at least one guest operating system under it. The performance of the guest system can depend on how paging is set up for that guest system and the release of VM that is installed.

Basic Set-Up

With VM and a guest system, like VSE, that itself uses dynamic address translation, the system could theoretically be set up so that VSE would page in and out in its usual way, and it in turn would be paged in and out of real storage. This would mean that a page of a processing program would be paged into the VSE area for processing, and would then be paged into VM's real storage for processing. This

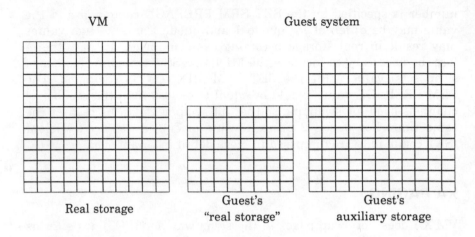

Figure 4-3   Double paging set-up.

is illustrated in Figure 4-3. The process is called double paging. It is obviously inefficient to move a page twice in order to process the instructions within it.

VM will build segment and page tables to translate from virtual addresses to real addresses. The guest operating system will itself build segment and page tables to translate addresses from virtual to what it considers to be real storage. S/370 hardware cannot handle a three-level address translation, although XA can. SP will, therefore, build shadow page tables that can be used to map from guest virtual addresses to real addresses.

Handshaking

Handshaking was introduced with VS1 and VSE as a way of giving a one-to-one match of guest real and guest virtual storage and thereby improve performance. Handshaking consists of the use of two techniques, nonpaging mode and pseudo page faults (see later).

Shadow Page Tables

Shadow page tables are used with SP and HPO and a guest operating system to map from guest virtual addresses to real addresses. They are constructed entry by entry as page faults occur for the guest system. This carries with it a performance overhead. When VM wants to steal a page from the guest, it knows which page of the guest it is stealing. Unfortunately, it does not know which entry in the shadow page table it has to invalidate and so it invalidates the whole shadow page table. As a consequence of this, when it redispatches the guest, it will revalidate the shadow page table entries one at a time as page faults occur.

With HPO the shadow page table revalidation process can be facilitated by the use of VMA (see Chapter 5). VMA microcode will recognize those potential page faults which do not mean that a page is nonresident but are caused by VM invalidating the entries in the shadow page table. VMA will turn off the invalid bit in the page table entry and allow execution to proceed. This obviously improves performance.

V=V Guest

One way to improve the performance of a V=V guest (i.e., one running in virtual storage) is to use a virtual address space that is equal to the virtual machine size. This is illustrated in Figure 4-4. If things are set up in this way, the guest system will not have to perform any paging itself. Therefore, this is sometimes called *nonpaging mode*. With VS1 and DOS/VS the guest builds segment and page tables which map one-to-one their virtual to real addresses. With early releases they ran with the Dynamic Address Translation (DAT) bit set, which forced VM to maintain shadow page tables. However, with later releases they did not turn the DAT bit on, which consequently improved performance. Also double Channel Command Word (CCW) translation was eliminated because the guest did not perform any CCW translation.

V=R Guest

It is possible to set up the system such that the guest system is in real storage with VM. This is called virtual equals real. The advantage of running in this mode is that the guest can be dispatched with its own segment and page tables, and VM does not need to build shadow page tables. If a guest is to run V=R, the commands SET NOTRANS ON and SET STBYPASS (see Chapter 6) are used to tell VM to bypass channel program translation and shadow page tables for this particular guest.

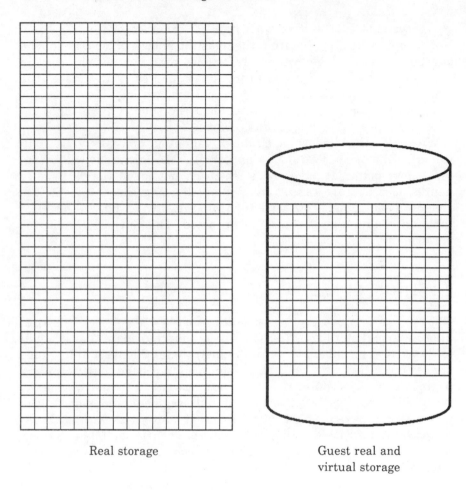

Real storage   Guest real and
                                virtual storage

Figure 4-4   Nonpaging mode.

Guest Page Faults

With guests running V=V, if VM tells the guest that a page fault has occurred at an address, the guest will dispatch another partition and continue processing to the end of its time slot. This is an example of a *pseudo page fault*. When VM has fetched the missing page, it informs the guest system using another pseudo page fault interrupt. The guest system is able to redispatch the original partition. This pseudo page fault handshaking is activated using the SET PAGEX ON command.

XA Set-Up

With XA it is possible to use expanded storage (where available) for paging. It is also possible to allocate blocks of 1 MB of expanded storage for guest systems running V=R or V=F to use for their paging.

Under XA, guest execution is not initiated by an LPSW instruction (as in 370 mode) but by a Start Interpretive Execution (SIE) instruction. SIE contains the address of the state descriptor control block. This control block contains, among other information, a descriptor of the guest system's mode, i.e., 370 or XA, and its timers.

Interpretive Execution   Interpretive execution is the name given to guest execution under SIE. It may stop for one of two reasons:

- An interrupt may occur. This is typically an I/O interrupt. CP would have to analyze it and pass control to the appropriate guest.
- The guest attempts something that the microcode cannot handle. This is called an intercept. In this case, execution of the SIE terminates and control passes to the next sequential instruction.

With XA there are no shadow tables because SIE can handle three-level address translation. Translations from guest virtual to guest real addresses are handled by the guest page tables. Guest real to host real address translation is handled by XA's page tables.

Because there are no shadow page tables to maintain, the guest sytems will perform much better under XA than under HPO.

Multiple High Performance Guests

The Multiple High Performance Guest (MHPG) feature is available with XA SP and allows up to six guest systems to get the performance benefits of SIE assists for dedicated devices. This allows one guest to run V=R (Virtual equals Real) and up to five guests to run V=F (Virtual equals Fixed).

PR/SM

The Processor Resource/System Manager feature available on some processors allows the processor to be divided into seven logical partitions. In a similar manner to MHPG, each partition (guest system) is allocated central storage, expanded storage, channels, and central processor. This simulation of the VM/XA MHPG feature makes use of SIE microcode. A guest system that is running in a dedicated partition does not come out of SIE mode when it goes into a wait state.

PAGING AND I/O

All paging I/O to auxiliary storage takes preference over other I/O activities. However, the one problem that many sites experience when looking at monitor statistics regarding paging activity is that the situation is complicated by the fact that spooling uses the same subsystem; and with SP and HPO, spooling statistics are included with paging statistics. PAGE and spool areas can be kept separate using format/allocate PAGE. If this is done, then separate information about spooling and paging can be obtained.

With XA there are four counters that can be used to separate paging and spooling activities. These are PLSPIOPR, PLSPIOPW, PLSPIOSR, and PLSPIOSW.

AUXILIARY STORAGE PERFORMANCE

Auxiliary storage contains the pages of virtual machines that are running under CP. It may be on disk or expanded storage or on solid state devices. Paging to expanded storage is preferred because it does not involve any external I/O and can be performed very quickly. With expanded storage, address resolution is at the page level, rather than at the segment and page level. VM/SP cannot use expanded storage.

Defining Page Areas

With SP, there are two types of areas that can be used for paging and can be specified by systems programmers. They are PAGE space and TEMP space and are specified using the SYSOWN macro. With HPO an additional SWAP area can be defined using the SYSPAG macro.

Paging Hierarchy

TEMP space is used mainly for spooling but can be used for paging if the PAGE space is filled up. If this happens, spooling I/O will interfere with paging and the situation should be avoided. SP will select the fastest device available that has been allocated as PAGE when paging out. If all the devices are of the same speed, SP will do one page-out in turn to each device in the order in which they are specified in SYSOWN. SYSOWN is a macro in DMKSYS. If two or more channels are to be used for paging, the devices should be specified in SYSOWN so as to alternate between channels.

With HPO, there are five levels in the hierarchy, and these can be determined by users with the SYSPAG macro. The five are:

- SW—swap area
- PP—preferred paging
- PG—general paging
- PM—page migration
- PS—spooling (this is used for overflow only)

With XA paging areas should be allocated across all available paths. The SYSCPVOL macro in HCPSYS is used to specify devices in the path rotation order that is required.

HPO Paging   Page-outs will go to PP devices. If PP devices are full, page-outs will go to PG; if PG are full to PM; and if PM are full to PS. If more than one SYSPAG macro is defined at any level, the devices on the first macro will be used until full, then those on each other macro in turn. Therefore, when adding new devices to the list of those available, the SYSPAG macro should not be duplicated; instead, new devices should be added to the existing macro. If the macro is duplicated, the expected performance improvements will not happen.

Device selection is the same as with SP except that several page-outs will take place to one device before moving to the next. This will allow block paging, i.e., multiple pages written at once, to take place. Page-in operations always take place one at a time. The number of pages that are written to a device at any one time depends on the device type. For cache devices and expanded storage the value is one. For 3380s the value is 10 (see Table 4-1).

Monitoring what is happening on preferred paging devices can be done by using the following commands:

Table 4-1   Number of pages per block used when paging.

Device type	Block size
3330	8
3340	3
3350	8
3370	3
3375	8
3380	10
3880-1	1

```
IND PAGING ALL
IND USER
Q SRM PGMACT
Q SRM MAXPP
```

With HPO, any changes can be made using the SET SRM MAXPP command.

HPO Swapping   Swapping will take place to SW devices unless they are full. In that case swapping will follow the paging hierarchy (i.e., PP, PG, PM, and PS, in that order). If a paging device is used, pages will be read back singly. In performance terms this loses all the benefits of swapping.

The SYSPAG macro specifies the swap set size and varies according to device type. For 3380s a value of 9 or 19 is used. It is set up as SYSPAG . . . , TYPE = SW, SWSIZE = nn where nn is the swap set size, e.g., 19.

The swap set size that is used should depend on the workload. If there are large working sets, large swap set sizes should be used.

The swap areas should be allocated on several paths to allow parallel swapping. Also, it is a good idea to rotate paths in the SYSPAG volume list.

At queue add time, a number of swap sets are swapped in. This number is specified in the SET SRM PREPAGE Q1 nn Q2 mm command. Swapping in should prevent page faults occurring. If a page fault does occur on a page that had been part of the working set, the swap set is swapped in. This should prevent any more page faults occuring for that swap set and thereby improve performance.

Selecting Page Slots

With SP the page slot that is nearest to the center of a device will be selected. This allows paging space to be overallocated, although only the required amount is used.

With HPO a moving cursor algorithm is used. This means that page slots are allocated according to the position of the cursor. The cursor itself moves forward from one end of a paging or swapping area and then back again. Using this method, contiguous space for block paging or swapping is more likely to be found. Because all parts of the paging area are likely to be used, care must be taken not to overallocate space that could lead to excessive head movement and deterioration in performance.

Page Migration

Page migration is the process by which pages are moved down the hierarchy of devices if a certain percentage of space at one level is full. The percentage can be specified in SP with the SET SRM MHFULL command and in HPO with SET SRM PGULL command.

In HPO, pages will be migrated from SW areas to PP only if they are on expanded storage or on cache devices. Also, with HPO, pages are never migrated to spool areas.

For optimum performance, page migration should only occur from expanded storage or solid state devices. Even so there is still a high performance penalty because every migrated page has to move through real storage.

PERFORMANCE CONSIDERATIONS

VM/SP

If all the PAGE areas that are allocated are small, this will reduce seek time and so improve response time. One PAGE area should be allocated near the middle of a pack. If 3380s are used, its size should be about 80 cylinders. When deciding on how many PAGE areas to set up, the general rule to follow is to allocate one per 3380 actuator for every 15 pages per second required. Paging packs should be allocated across as many control units and channels as possible to avoid contention. The SYSOWN macro should be used to specify CP-owned volumes in an order that rotates the access around all the DASD paths. Performance will deteriorate dramatically if TEMP areas are used for paging.

VM/SP HPO

There is little point in trying to allocate more than one of each of PAGE, SWAP, and spool areas on a pack because the additional one will not be used until the first one is full up. PAGE and SWAP areas should be allocated near the middle of a pack and kept small in size to reduce seek times. The recommended size for PAGE areas is 60 cylinders; for SWAP areas it is 120 cylinders. As many control units and channels as possible should be used to avoid contention. The SYSPAG macro can be used to ensure that PAGE and SWAP areas are used in an order that rotates access around the different paths available. The default values for the SYSPAG macro should not be used. There is a performance overhead in paging to TEMP areas and this should always be avoided.

VM/XA SP

With XA as with other systems it is important to spread the load around as many channel paths (CHPs) as possible. The SYSCPVOL macro in HCPSYS can be used to specify the devices in the path rotation order that is required.

USEFUL SET COMMANDS

There are a number of SET commands that can be used to improve the performance of virtual machines in the area of paging. Full details are given in Chapter 6, but a summary follows:

LOCK—locks a specified number of a user's pages in storage.

SET MINWS—used with HPO to ensure that a minimum number of pages are always included in the working set and put on the swap queues.

SET QDROP OFF—prevents a user's pages from going through the usual queue drop processing.

SET RESERVE—reserves page frames for a specified user.

SET SRM MINNUMSS—specifies a minimum number of page frames that are to be available for page-ins and swap-ins.

SET SRM PREPAGE—specifies the number of swap sets to be swapped in when a user is added to the the swap queue.

SET SRM SWPQTIME—specifies the length of time a user spends on each swap queue.

SET SRM MHFULL (SP)
SET SRM PGULL (HPO)—specifies the percentage of space on a device that is to be full before page migration will take place.

SET SRM MAXDRUM (SP)
SET SRM MAXPP (HPO)—specifies the maximum number of page slots that can be occupied by one user in the preferred paging area (fixed-load paging area with SP).

HINTS AND TIPS

The following are some hints and tips about devices and paging.

- The fastest devices available should be used.
- Fixed head devices or solid state devices (expanded storage or cache controllers) should be used for preferred paging space. This is because demand page-ins are carried out a page at a time; therefore, the overhead of DASD seek times and rotational delay significantly affect performance.

- Placing swap areas on DASD does not cause significant performance problems. This is because swapping involves blocks of pages; therefore, the DASD overhead is not so significant.
- The usual I/O tuning rules apply to paging and swapping devices. Enough devices and paths should be used to ensure good response. An extra consideration with swapping devices is that they should be spread over a number of channels to allow for simultaneous prepaging of swap sets.
- TEMP areas should never be used for paging—although paging into the TEMP area will prevent the system from crashing.
- The number of virtual channels, virtual control units, and virtual devices defined in users' directory entries should be kept to a minimum. This will reduce the number of virtual control blocks created and stored in the free storage area. This should reduce the number of free storage extends and keep more DPA space available.
- Expanded storage or cached 3880s are best used for page areas and 3380s for swapping areas. With HPO and XA, paging rates can be reduced by using expanded storage.
- PAGE space should be placed near the center of the the disk but should not be spread across the center. The center is considered to be zero and addresses run either side of it. If the PAGE area is either side of the center, it increases seek time.
- Paging and spooling always take precedence over other I/O. If S and Y disks are placed on the same packs as either paging or spooling, the response to CMS users will be greatly inhibited.
- If plenty of memory is available, there will be no paging and this in itself will improve performance.
- HPO will perform I/O to the paging areas in the order in which they are specified in the SYSPAG macro of DMKSYS. If multiple channels are in use, the volume names as specified should alternate on a channel basis.
- Movement of pages backward and forward between central storage and expanded storage is synchronous. This means that processing stops until the transfer is complete. However, the process is much faster than paging and, therefore, overall performance is not impaired. Address resolution within expanded storage is at the page level.

5

Assists

An assist is microcode that may be incorporated in the hardware of some CPU models. The availability of certain facilities depends on the processor model and the microcode level installed. It is always worth checking that the processor installed or to be purchased has the required assists available. This may assume even greater importance with non-IBM processors. When an assist is used it will perform certain instructions, thus saving CP from performing them. This will typically result in the time taken to perform an instruction being reduced, thus giving a consequent improvement in performance. It is typically the more frequently used instructions that are worthwhile microcoding. In the past, when performance problems have been reported, it has been known for assists not to have been turned on, and this was often the first thing to check when trying to identify the cause of a problem.

The assists covered in this chapter are:

- VMA
- ECPS
- CPA
- EVMA
- VITA
- IUCV assist
- STBA

- PMA
- PMAV
- SIE assist

VMA

Virtual Machine Assist (VMA) was the first of the assists introduced by IBM. It was introduced because the operating systems that were newly available at that time (e.g., VS1 or DOS/VS) were performing much slower under VM than when run native. The reason for this was simply that the new 370 operating systems were making a lot of use of the new privileged operations. Using VMA reduces the time taken to execute a privileged operation considerably. For example, the time taken to execute SSK and LRA instructions without VMA is about 50 microseconds. With VMA the time is reduced to about 5 microseconds. This is illustrated in Figure 5-1. VMA is managed by the MICBLOCK control block.

Privileged Operations

Privileged operations (privops) account for just less than 25 percent of the system/370 repertoire. When a guest system tries to use a privileged operation, a privileged operation exception is taken and CP is given control. CP will simulate the effect of the privop and then redispatch the virtual machine.

The privop count in VMMAP reports may not be accurate because it does not count some instructions.

MICBLOCK

The MICBLOCK is a special control block that manages VMA. It is set up by the software and is pointed to by Control Register 6. At the moment when a privop exception would be taken, the MICBLOCK is examined by the microcode to see if:

- The guest is in virtual supervisor state.
- The privop can be handled by VMA without taking the program interrupt.

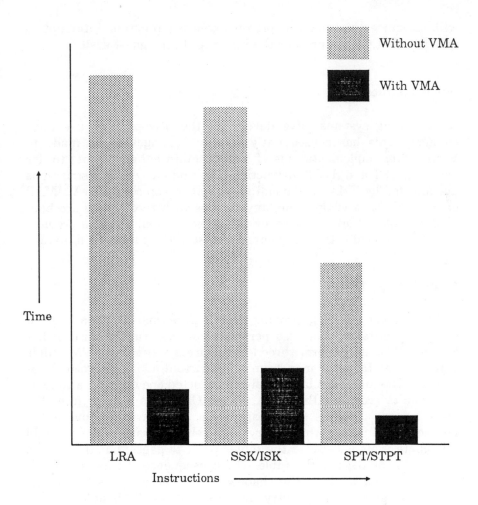

Figure 5-1   Performance improvements using VMA.

VMA CP Interrelationship

VM always contains the software to perform the same activities as are performed by VMA in case the VMA function is not available. One of the results of this is that VMA needs only handle the most common uses of the privop. For example, if a guest system uses the STOSM instruction to enable for interrupts, it is typically handled by VMA. However, if there is an interrupt pending for the guest, VMA will recognize this and the privop exception program interrupt is taken so that CP can present the interrupt to the guest system.

Which Instructions?

As operating systems have developed, the privops they use have changed. This has consequently required changes to be made to VMA. Later implementations of VMA contain enhancements to, for example, SPT and STPT instructions. To find out which instructions are assisted by VMA, it is usual to look at privop counts in VMMAP or SMART. Most of the time, any privops with zero counts are handled by VMA or are not used by the guest system. The one problem with this method is that it ignores the instructions that it simulates.

Shadow Page Tables

VMA is important in improving overall performance when a guest system is installed that also performs address translation. Neither SP nor HPO can perform three-level address translation. VM builds shadow page tables to map from guest virtual addresses to real addresses. The tables are laboriously constructed one entry at a time as page faults occur for the guest. When CP steals a page from the guest system, it knows which page of the guest it is stealing, but it has no way of telling which entry in the shadow page table it should invalidate. This is because the tables point to pages, but there is no pointer in the page to the table. The consequence of this is that CP invalidates the whole of the shadow page table and has to start to rebuild it again entry by entry. The VMA microcode is able to identify those potential page faults caused by the shadow page table being invalidated even though the page is still in real storage. VMA turns off the invalid bit in the shadow page table and execution is allowed to proceed.

VMA and CMS

Because CMS is an operating system and issues many privileged instructions, e.g., LPSW, SSK, SSM, etc., which can be performed by the microcode, there is a performance advantage to CMS in having VMA running.

ECPS

The Extended Control Support Program was introduced after VMA. It was introduced after work had been done to find ways to improve VM's performance on intermediate machines. It is not available on 3080s and 3090s. It can improve overall VM performance by up to as much as 50 percent. It has three components:

• CPA
• EVMA
• VITA

CPA

The Control Program Assist contains single instructions to replace the most frequently used CP instructions. The new instructions are invoked by op-codes in the form of X'E6nn'. Because the instructions are run in microcode form they are much faster than their Assembler counterparts. If VM is run on old machines without the assist, it will run because VM still contains Assembler versions of the instructions. At IPL time CP will overwrite the E6 instructions with No-op instructions, and control will pass to the old code.

EVMA

The Extended Virtual Machine Assist assists more privileged operations than VMA. It also allows partial assists for those instructions that the assist cannot handle completely.

VITA

The Virtual Interval Timer Assist is used to ensure that a virtual machine's interval timer is maintained with an accuracy similar to that of the real system's interval timer. This assist is relatively unimportant with the current generation of operating systems because most use the more accurate System/370 CPU timer for accounting purposes. However, timing had been a large problem with older systems.

IUCV ASSIST

The IUCV (Inter-User Communication Vehicle) assist is used to improve both VM/VTAM performance and SFS (Shared File System) performance. It is available on 4381 and 9370 processors.

STBA

The Shadow Table Bypass Assist is available on some CPUs, for example, the 4381. It improves performance by handling in microcode those instructions that would be performed by CP. The instructions concerned are those necessary to handle guests with multiple address spaces, e.g., MVS. The most outstanding of the instructions is LCTL, which is used to switch address spaces. The STBA is invoked by the SET STBYPASS VR command.

PMA

The Preferred Machine Assist was introduced to enable MVS users to attain near native performance when running under VM/SP HPO. Its effect is to reduce the VM overhead. It has recently been extended to include VSE systems.

With PMA active, control will pass to CP for a guest system in one of only three conditions. These are:

• At the end of a timeslice
• When an interrupt is received from a device on a VM channel
• When the guest system goes into a wait state

How It Works

PMA is an extension of V=R support allowing the preferred guest to be dispatched in what is almost real supervisor state. By omitting channels from the VM SYSGEN they can be designated as PMA channels. The preferred guest can drive I/O to, and receive interrupts from, those channels without any VM overhead. Internally, all but a few occasional privileged instructions can be executed by the preferred guest without incurring any VM overhead.

Difficulties

It should be pointed out that there are addressing rules about the configuration of PMA guests. Because some sites are unable to conform to these constraints, they cannot make use of the PMA option.

PMAV

The PMAV is an extension to PMA. It allows guests running under VM to not only gain all the advantages available through using PMA, but also to issue VM commands using DIAGNOSE. A guest running under VM with only PMA does not know it is a guest under VM. Therefore, if it tries to communicate with VM using the Diagnose interface, the command will be executed by the hardware. This will most likely lead to unpredictable and unwanted results. To indicate to the guest system that it is a PMAV guest, CP will return a response starting X'FF' to a Store CPU-id instruction issued by the guest.

SIE ASSIST

The Start Interpretive Execution assist was introduced with VM/XA. A guest operating system is started by an SIE instruction. This points to the state descriptor control block. The control block contains all the information that the SIE assist might conceivably ever need to know about the guest system.

Performance Improvements

The SIE assist automatically handles three-level address translation. This means that guest virtual to guest real address translations are handled using the guest system's page tables. Guest system real to XA real address translation is handled by XA's page tables. There is no longer a requirement to build and maintain shadow page tables for guests who, like MVS, have multiple address spaces. As a consequence of this saving, MVS will perform better under XA than under HPO. This is illustrated in Figure 5-2.

The SIE assist reduces the overhead of I/O instructions issued by the preferred guest to dedicated devices. Dedication is at the device level rather than, as in HPO PMA, at the channel level. Another

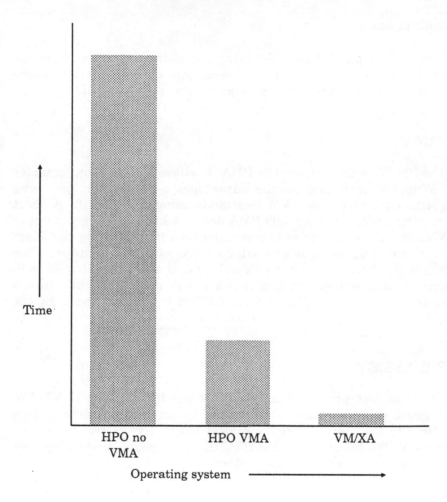

Figure 5-2   Performance improvements using VM/XA.

benefit of this is that XA is much easier to configure than HPO with a PMA guest.

XA in conjunction with the PR/SM feature of 3090 machines allows up to a maximum of seven preferred guests to be running concurrently. All seven will get the benefit of the SIE assist for dedicated devices.

Most future work on assists by IBM is likely to be associated with SIE assists.

6

The SET Commands

The SET commands can be used once the VM system is up and running to modify the way that work is to be processed. It should always be borne in mind that when a command is used, it may have a beneficial effect on one part of the system; i.e., there may be performance improvements for a CMS user or for a guest system. This, however, may result in a degradation in the service offered to another part of the system, i.e., response times for PROFS users. Some of the commands may be specified on the option statement in a user's entry in the system directory. Alternatively, the commands themselves may be keyed in by authorized users, automatically entered by AUTOLOG, or specified in a user's PROFILE EXEC.

WHO CAN USE SET COMMANDS

The SET commands considered in this chapter all have an effect on overall machine performance and are, therefore, frequently restricted to authorized users. These authorized users are typically the systems programmers, the operator, AUTOLOG, and the technical support group. It is important that if systems programmers or technical support make changes to a parameter, they inform the other people concerned with performance and maintaining service level agreements; otherwise, chaos can ensue as each group of people separately make modifications that contradict each other.

COMMAND FORMAT

The command format for using SET commands is generally:

```
SET nnnn   ON/OFF
```

or

```
SET nnnn user-id xx
```

where

```
nnnn = command
xx = a value
```

It should be remembered that some commands that work with SP do not work with HPO or XA releases or may do so in different ways. Therefore, it is worth checking with the manual to find what command formats are available for the version of VM installed.

COMMANDS INCLUDED

The SET commands covered in this chapter are:

- SET RESERVE
- SET QDROP
- SET MINWS
- SET SRM
- SET PRIORITY
- SET FAVOR
- SET QUICKDSP
- SET SHARE
- SET PAGEX
- SET PAGING
- SET STBYPASS
- SET STMULTI
- SET REMOTE
- SET BMX
- SET 370E
- SET AUTOPOLL
- SET AFFINITY

• SET IOASSIST
• SET MAXUSER

Also included in this chapter are details of the LOCK command, included here because there is a similarity between its use and function and some SET commands.

SET RESERVE

The effect of the SET RESERVE command is to reserve a number of page frames in real storage. This number of pages will be maintained in storage, and will always be allocated to the user-id even if his working set size falls below that number. It acts as a private page pool for that user.

Command Format

The format of the command is:

```
SET RESERVE user-id xx
```

where user-id is a virtual machine and xx is a number.

With SP the command can only be issued for one user-id. With HPO and XA the command can be issued for any number of users.

Reasons for Using Command

One sensible use for the SET RESERVE command is to retain a number of pages for a user in storage while the user is inactive, so that when the user-id becomes active again its response time will be as good as before. A real life example would be a heavily used interactive system running under VM. During the morning it will typically retain its working set resident in DPA. This will consequently lead to good response times being experienced by the interactive users. However, at lunch time the transaction rate on the system will drop dramatically as users break from work. The system will tend to reallocate the working set pages to other users. At the end of the lunch period the interactive users will start work again, but because their pages are no longer in storage, response times will suffer while the working set is reestablished in real storage.

The most frequently reserved user-ids are guest operating systems and server machines.

What Happens

With VM/SP, when the SET RESERVE command has been issued for a single user-id, the first pages in storage referenced by that user will be flagged as reserved until the number specified in the command is reached. All future core table scans will automatically bypass the page frames occupied by these pages. The exception to this rule is when a frame is required by the reserved user.

With VM/SP HPO the command can be issued for any number of users. When the command is issued it will only reserve working set pages. This means that trimming will still occur. Page stealing can occur from reserved pages by a core table scan on its second pass if no other page frames can be found.

Problems Experienced

When using the command on an SP system, care must be taken as to when the command is issued. The problem experienced is that the pages reserved are not necessarily the ones that are most required. If the command is issued at IPL time, it is the IPL code that tends to get reserved, which is no use to the system once it is running.

With HPO and XA, the problem is that reserved pages are stolen after a second scan of the core table reveals that there are no other unused pages.

The more pages that are reserved for a particular user-id, the fewer pages that are left in the common page pool (with the DPA) for all the other active users to make use of. This may cause the other virtual machines to page at an unacceptable rate.

Solutions

With SP the sensible approach is not to issue the SET command around the time of IPL, but to wait until the system is up and running. In the case of a VSE system it would generally be best to wait until the main system running under VSE (probably CICS) had started and then to issue the SET RESERVE command. Another option is to periodically issue SET RESERVE OFF commands followed by the usual SET RESERVE.

With HPO and XA in order to ensure that the required number of pages are kept in the DPA, the SET MINWS (see later) command should be used at the same time.

It should be noted that HPO and XA do not experience the same problem as SP because with these systems the active pages are retained. Therefore, if the composition of the working set changes over a period of time, the active pages will still be retained.

To prevent excessive paging of other systems because too many pages have been reserved, it is important to make use of monitors that are available. Both VMMAP and SMART (VMRTM) give an average working set value which could be used as a starting value. This value can be modified and the difference in overall performance noted. Using this information another change can be made. It is worth remembering the golden rule of applying changes, which is "one thing at a time." This is the only way of knowing what change had an effect.

It may be the case that SET RESERVE can improve the performance of an important busy live system (e.g., CICS under VSE) and decrease it on less important systems (e.g., test VSE). This trade-off is one that is often considered realistic.

SET QDROP

The SET QDROP command can be used to reduce the amount of paging that takes place for a particular user-id. The command will eliminate queue dropping for that virtual machine. Therefore, the pages in real storage for that user will remain there.

Command Format

The command format is:

```
SET QDROP user-id OFF/ON
```

where user-id is the virtual machine to be affected by the command.

Reasons for Using Command

The command can retain pages in real storage when they would otherwise be flushed out. The reasons for using it are similar to those for using SET RESERVE. An interactive system would have to give up page frames in real storage during quiet periods (e.g., lunch times). When the quiet period was over, users would not get such a good response as they were used to, while the system built up the working set size. By having the pages locked in real storage, the users will retain their response times even after extended periods of absence.

Typically it would be CICS in a VSE guest, or server machines (e.g., VTAM or PVM), that would benefit most from this command. It has been found, for example, that the use of the SET QDROP OFF command for SQL/DS not only decreased system page rates, but also allowed an increase in transaction rates.

It has also been reported that using the command on users with high paging rates not only reduced their paging (as expected from the command), but also dramatically reduced the system paging rate. The reason may be the effect of trimming hurting very large working sets by removing all pages not touched in the last queue stay.

What Happens

The effect of the command is different in SP and HPO.

With VM/SP the use of SET QDROP OFF will prevent the usual queue-drop processing being applied to a particular user's pages. During a core table scan the user's pages are always treated as if they belonged to an in-queue user. They are never all placed on the flushlist when the user becomes inactive, i.e., dropped from the queue.

With HPO (up to release 5) the effect of the SET QDROP OFF command is different in that it prevents trimming from taking place.

Problems Experienced

The main problem experienced with this command is that although one user may benefit, other users show a decrease in performance, and it is often difficult to predict what the outcome of using the command will be. Indeed, it is true that many sites warn operators and junior systems programmers about its use, while other sites ban its use altogether. It is also thought that indiscriminate use of the command might create problems with the storage management code.

Solutions

Many sites solve the problems associated with SET QDROP OFF by not using it at all. A more appropriate solution is to use it only for user-ids that can benefit and monitor what effect the command has had on the system as a whole. As was noted earlier, the effect can be surprisingly good for large virtual machines or large working set APL users, as well as SQL/DS, VTAM, and Passthrough.

SET MINWS

The SET MINWS command is not available to SP users. It specifies a minimum value for the working set size that the scheduler will use. It can be applied to a single user or to the system as a whole. The use of this command should help to reduce the number of page faults experienced by a user and thereby improve performance. It is often used in preference to the SET QDROP OFF command.

Command Format

The format of the command is:

```
SET MINWS system/user-id xx
```

where xx is a numeric value for the working set size, user-id is a single user, and system refers to the whole system. The default value for xx is double the swap set size.

Reasons for Using Command

The command is used to improve performance either of individual users or of the system in general. With untuned HPO 4.2 systems, the SET MINWS SYSTEM command can be used to increase a user's working set size. This will include pages that would otherwise have been paged in by demand paging. By having large working set sizes the system is forced to perform swapping, which, in fact, it is very good at although somewhat reluctant to carry out. There are obvious performance improvements to be gained from swapping rather than demand paging. It is worth noting that HPO release 5 does tend to swap more readily, and this may make the use of the SET MINWS command less necessary. However, there are still benefits from using it for individual virtual machines, in particular service machines.

What Happens

The effect is to increase the minimum working set size either for a particular user or on a system-wide basis. This means that the system will ensure that a minimum number of pages are always included in the working set regardless of whether they have been referenced. These pages may then be put in the swap queues. When a user starts working again after a break, the pages can be made available almost immediately by swapping in a block from the swap set.

Problems Experienced

There are no significant problems associated with this command, unless values that are completely different from SET RESERVE values are used, which can "confuse" the machine.

SET SRM

The SET SRM commands allow values to be passed to the System Resource Manager (SRM). These commands offer the ability to exercise some degree of control over memory management. They also permit some control over the allocation of memory.

Command Format

The formats of the commands that are useful are:

- SET SRM MINNUMSS nn
- SET SRM SWPQTIME intuser-id time nonintuser-id time
- SET SRM IBUF bufftime tt maxsize nn
- SET SRM MAXPP nn

- SET SRM APAGES nn
- SET SRM MAXWSS nn
- SET SRM STORBUF nn% mm% pp%
- SET SRM DSPBUF nn mm pp
- SET SRM LDUBUF nn% mm% pp%
- SET SRM IABIAS nn% mm
- SET SRM PREPAGE Q1 xx Q2 yy
- SET SRM PGULL nn

Reasons for Using Commands

The MINNUMSS command specifies the minimum number of swap sets that are in use, and its effect is to ensure that a specified number of page frames are always available for page-ins and swap-ins. This can speed up the paging-in and swapping-in activity and thus improve performance overall.

With HPO the SWPQTIME command can be used to specify how long (in minutes) an interactive and noninteractive user can keep a page frame in storage before it becomes a candidate for swapping out. The default value of 20 seconds is usually retained for interactive users, but the value for noninteractive users is usually reduced from 100 to around 5. With HPO release 5 the command was removed.

The IBUF command controls both the size and the duration of residence in the interactive buffer. This command can be used to strike a balance between interactive and batch work. When the value for the interactive buffer is reduced, additional page frames become available for production jobs. If interactive performance is poor, the buffer size can be increased, thus providing users with better response times.

The MAXPP command (not available with SP) specifies the percentage of the preferred paging area that may become full before automatic page migration is invoked (or control the number of page slots which can be occupied by one user in the preferred paging area). It has been found that with HPO 4.3 systems, reducing this value will cause it to start migrating pages. If page migration is taking place, this command should be used to stop large users from causing the preferred paging area to fill up. SET SRM MAXDRUM has the same effect in SP for fixed-load paging areas.

The APAGES command can be used on SP systems to tell the scheduler how many page frames are to be used for the calculation of available page frames. If a low number is used this will reduce paging and reduce the multiprogramming level. If a high number is used it will result in an increase in paging rates and a higher multiprogramming level.

The MAXWSS can be used with SP to specify the maximum number of pages in a user's working set that the scheduler will consider in its calculations. However, it does not actually restrict the number of pages used. What it does is create pages that the scheduler cannot see.

With XA, STORBUF can be used to specify what proportion of storage is available to all classes of user (Q1, Q2, and Q3). It can also be used to specify the upper limit of usage by Q2 and Q3 users or to specify the maximum to be available to Q3 users only. The command is primarily used to control paging rates. For example, in a situation where the IND Q command shows that there are users in the eligible list (Ex) and paging rates are low, it is worth considering overcommitting main storage by using a value above 100 percent.

With XA, the DSPBUF parameter can be used to put a limit on the number of each type of user that is to be allowed onto the queue at once. Its main application is at sites that have a large number of heavy concurrent users and where the most significant bottleneck problems are with I/O rather than storage. The command can be used to limit the number of concurrent heavy users and this may improve overall throughput of work.

With XA, the LDUBUF parameter controls the number of heavy paging users that the system will allow. It is not a very sensitive parameter value to code because it works by assessing how many paging actuators each user will utilize. Therefore, its main application is at sites where there are a large number of paging volumes installed.

The IABIAS command can be used to benefit interactive users. Again, this command is only available with XA. It can be used to specify by how much the performance of interactive users should be improved in addition to what their share would be.

The PREPAGE command can be used to specify the number of swap sets that are to be paged in when a user is added to the swap queue. A different value can be specified for queue 1 and queue 2 users. If too high a value is specified, real storage may become overcommitted. The value should not be higher than the number of channels used for swapping so that all swap sets can be read at the same time. For queue 2 users a value of one is usually sufficient. If the PREPAGE value is increased, it is necessary to ensure that enough page frames are available. It may, therefore, be necessary to increase the MINNUMSS value using the SET SRM MINNUMSS nn command.

The PGULL command is used with HPO to specify how full (i.e., a percentage value) a paging device is to become before page migration will automatically take place. For SP users the command to use is MHFULL.

SET PRIORITY

The SET PRIORITY command can be used to alter the priority (but not the deadline priority directly) of a user-id. The effect of this will be to either improve or reduce the performance of the specified virtual machine.

Command Format

The format of the command is:

```
SET PRIORITY user-id xx
```

where xx is a value in the range of 1 to 99 with 1 being a higher (i.e., yielding better performance) value.

Reasons for Using Command

Giving a user a low number priority (i.e., nearer one) means that a virtual machine is more likely to be selected for dispatch when sitting on the queue waiting. This in turn means that the user will experience an improvement in performance. It is a command quite frequently entered by operators to speed up the throughput rate for a particular virtual machine.

What Happens

The default directory entry for any user's priority is 64. When the user-id is active on the system it will be dispatched according to its deadline priority. The value of the deadline priority is linked to the user priority by a complex formula (more fully discussed in Chapter 3). The deadline priority is calculated by the scheduler every time that a virtual machine finishes being dispatched (i.e., at queue drop). This means that the figure is recalculated whenever the virtual machine is waiting for some event to occur. The deadline priority is calculated using values for the user priority, the virtual machine resource consumption, time of day when the user was last dispatched, and the global system load. Changing the user priority with the SET PRIORITY command will indirectly affect the value of the deadline priority. It is worth noting that the use of a deadline priority prevents a single virtual machine with a high priority monopolizing the CPU.

Problems Experienced

There are generally few problems with this command. However, it has been known on occasion for its use to get a little out of hand, where authorized users have raised the priority of a couple of userids out of all proportion to the overall workflow through the system.

The other problem that can occur is caused by the fact that the command appears to be aimed at a specific target, but really is not. Many people do not appreciate the complex nature of the relationship between user priority and deadline priority and may be a little surprised at the outcome.

Solutions

Training and management seem to be the main answers to these problems. Provided people are fully aware of what the effects of the command are and appreciate the effect of its compulsive and indiscriminate use, this should avoid serious abuse. Good management would ensure that suitable training was available and also watch out for anyone using SET PRIORITY incorrectly.

With training, people would not only fully appreciate the command's effects, but might realize that the problem they are trying to remedy by using SET PRIORITY could be better solved using some other approach.

SET FAVOR

The SET FAVOR command can be used to improve the performance experienced by a virtual machine. It will do one of two things:

- Ensure that when a virtual machine is ready to run, its user-id is put in the run list, i.e., that it is on the list of dispatchable machines
- Ensure that a user-id is given a specified percentage of CPU—if it can use it

Command Format

The format of the command is:

```
SET FAVOR user-id
```

or

```
SET FAVOR user-id xx
```

where xx stands for a percentage value of CPU use and user-id is the name of a virtual machine. The percentage value specified can be between 1 and 100. 100 is a special case, in that it means VM will always try to dispatch that virtual machine first.

Reasons for Using Command

This command is used to improve the performance of a given virtual machine. FAVOR is arguably the most precise means of controlling CPU consumption and is typically used in preference to many of the other SET commands examined in this chapter, although it can be used in conjunction with SET PRIORITY, in which case it is imperative that sensible values are used for each.

What Happens

When the SET FAVOR command is used without the percentage option the user-id specified is placed on the queue whenever it is ready to run. The usual system code that checks to see if the working set will fit into storage is bypassed.

With the percentage option specified the scheduler will try to give the specified virtual machine that percentage of system CPU resource. If a user has used more than the specified percentage, he will have to compete on an equal basis with other virtual machines. If the virtual machine is unable to use all the allotted percentage during one queue stay, it is not necessarily given a higher priority next time.

If the percentages specified for a number of different user-ids exceed 100 percent, the control program will reduce the values proportionately.

Problems Experienced

With any given system a particular virtual machine may get more or less than the percentage value specified. If the command is used in conjunction with the SET PRIORITY command for a particular user, the values specified for both must change the performance of the virtual machine in the same direction; i.e., they must both improve or reduce performance. If the values conflict, the PRIORITY value will tend to be taken more into consideration by the system, and, therefore, the expected results of the SET FAVOR command will not occur.

Solutions

Again, the solution to the problem is to ensure that people using the command are fully aware of the implications of its use and that some form of check is made to ensure that the appropriate percentage values are entered and that no other conflicting command is being entered.

SET QUICKDSP

The SET QUICKDSP command is the XA equivalent of the SET FAVOR command.

Command Format

The format of the command is:

```
SET QUICKDSP user-id
```

Reasons for Using Command

The command is used in the XA environment in the situations in which the SET FAVOR command (without the percentage) would be used in a non-XA environment. It should improve the performance of a given virtual machine.

What Happens

Once the command is invoked for a particular user-id, that virtual machine will bypass the queue for storage availability. This will, therefore, improve its performance. The user is explicitly recognized as being in queue 1.

SET SHARE

SET SHARE is an XA command that is equivalent to two non-XA commands. With the ABS percentage option it is the equivalent of the non-XA SET FAVOR xx percent command. With the REL option it is similar to the SET PRIORITY command.

Command Format

The format of the command is:

```
SET SHARE user-id REL/ABS percent
```

where REL or ABS percent can be used for a given user-id.

Reasons for Using Command

The command is used in the XA environment when either SET
FAVOR user-id xx or SET PRIORITY user-id xx would be used in a
non-XA environment.

What Happens

The ABS percent option specifies a user's share of the CPU, storage,
and paging resources. (With XA SF it is just CPU.) Values for ABS
can add up to a maximum of 99 percent. If the values specified
should exceed that number, all the specified values are proportionately decreased until their sum is 99.

The REL value refers to the amount of CPU, storage, and paging
resource that is left after the ABS allocations have been subtracted.
This is why ABS values cannot exceed 99, otherwise there would be
no resources left for non-ABS virtual machines. The amount of resource that is allocated to non-ABS users is proportional to their
REL value.

SET PAGEX

The SET PAGEX command is used to enhance the relationship between VM and a guest operating system. In essence it greatly enhances the way paging is carried out between the two systems.

Command Format

The format of the command is:

```
SET PAGEX ON/OFF
```

Reasons for Using Command

The command is typically invoked automatically when a guest system such as VSE is IPLed. If it is not SET ON, a page fault occurring in a partition of VSE guest will in fact cause the VSE guest

itself to go into a wait state. When PAGEX is ON a page fault in a partition of a guest operating system will cause that partition only to go into a wait state. The guest system itself will continue multiprogramming in the usual way up to the end of its time slot.

What Happens

The SET PAGEX ON command activates pseudo page fault handling. A pseudo page fault occurs when VM tells a guest operating system that a page fault has occurred at a particular address. The guest system would identify this as a pseudo page fault and would dispatch another partition. When the missing page had been paged in by VM, VM would indicate this to the guest system using a different page fault interrupt. The original partition would then be available to be dispatched by the guest system.

If, when the first pseudo page fault occurs, the guest system does not have any other partitions to dispatch, it will sit and wait until VM has paged in the required page.

Problems Experienced

The only real problem with this is when ICCF is used under VSE/AF version 1. In order for ICCF to work properly in certain situations, it issues a SET PAGEX OFF command when it is started.

Solutions

The solution is to install VSE/SP 2.1 or later release. With this, ICCF only issues SET PAGEX OFF instructions as required and then issues a SET PAGEX ON command. The SET PAGEX OFF command is not issued when ICCF is started with later releases.

SET PAGING

The SET PAGING command is available with SP as a way of controlling the paging rate. It will also, as a consequence of its action, control the multiprogramming rate.

Command Format

The format of the command is:

    SET PAGING nn

where nn is a numerical value.

Reasons for Using Command

The command can be used in two quite different circumstances. If very high paging rates are observed, it is possible to enter a low value. This will reduce the paging rate.

The second use of the command would be in circumstances where a new paging device had been installed and it was considered that the system could stand higher paging rates. In this case a higher value would be entered.

What Happens

In both cases the value entered is used as a threshold value by CP. The system will modify the multiprogramming level so that the paging rate will be just below the threshold. Depending on how the system is set up, this can improve performance.

SET STBYPASS

The SET STBYPASS command is used to reduce the amount of activity that takes place, and the amount of resource required to do it, when an old set of shadow tables are flushed out and a new set are created. It is used for guest operating systems. It can only be used provided the STFIRST directory option is used. The command is only available with SP and HPO. XA does not build shadow page tables because it uses the SIE instruction (see Chapter 4).

Command Format

The format of the command is:

```
SET  STBYPASS  VR
SET  STBYPASS  nnK
```

Reasons for Using Command

The command can be used to improve the performance of a guest operating system. The first command is used for guests running V=R. The second command is used for guests running V=V.

What Happens

If the guest system is running V=R there is no point in VM building shadow page tables because the guest can be dispatched using its own segment and page tables. VM saves resources by not creating shadow page tables. If the command SET STBYPASS VR is issued on a 4381, it will also invoke the Shadow Table Bypass Assist (STBA) (see Chapter 5). STBA will handle the instructions necessary to look after multiple address space guest systems, in particular the LCTL instruction used to switch address spaces. Great savings can be achieved by having processing performed at the microcode level, and this manifests itself as overall performance improvements.

The SET STBYPASS nnK command can be used when a guest system such as MVS is run V=V. One of the characteristics of MVS/SP is that it is divided into three parts. The top part is called the common area and the bottom part is called the system or nucleus area. This is illustrated in Figure 6-1. These areas are shared by all address spaces. MVS dispatches multiple private areas which make up the address space and VM would need to keep a shadow page table for each private area. Because of the space that this would require it is not done. VM keeps only a limited number of such tables. When a new address space is dispatched VM attempts to find the shadow page table corresponding to that address space. If VM is unsuccessful, it flushes out an old set of tables and creates a new set. Because all MVS address spaces are identical up to a certain ad-

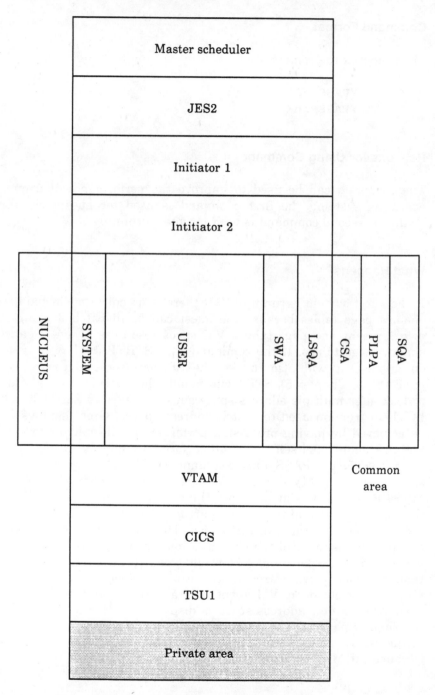

Figure 6-1   Example of MVS/SP address space layout.

dress, it is wasteful to flush out a table and build a new table that contains, in part, the same contents. By specifying a particular address this indicates to VM that it need not build shadow page tables for that part of the guest's address space.

Problems Experienced

The main problem is knowing how big to make the nnK value.

Solutions

The solution is to specify a very high value once the machine has been running for a while. When the command is issued, CP will reject it and specify the maximum acceptable value. This value can then be used. If the command is issued immediately after an IPL, the value may be artificially high.

SET STMULTI

The SET STMULTI command can be used to improve the performance of a guest operating system running V=V under SP or HPO. XA does not use shadow tables.

Command Format

The format of the command is:

```
SET STMULTI nn USEG mm CSEG pp
```

where nn, mm, and pp are numerical values. The nn value determines how many preallocated shadow page tables to keep for each address space. The USEG value specifies the number of segments for MVS private areas. The CSEG value specifies the size (in segments) of the CSA for MVS or SSA for VSE.

Reasons for Using Command

The command can be used with any operating system that has multiple address spaces, e.g., MVS. It can be used to specify the number of shadow page tables that are to be maintained for a guest. The more tables that are maintained, the less time that will be lost while tables are flushed out and new ones built. It is usually thought that for MVS the optimum nn value to use is the maximum of 16.

What Happens

The nn value specified tells VM how many address spaces should have their shadow tables retained in storage. The default value is 3, the maximum value is 16. The USEG value specified is usually the average size of a user region (MVS private area) measured in segments. The CSEG value is the size of the MVS common area. The optimum CSEG value can be found by mapping the storage of MVS or VSE from within those operating systems. The use of the CSEG command means that VM saves on resources by retaining common shadow page tables for all address spaces for the CSA area.

Problems Experienced

The problem that can occur when using this command is that the more shadow page tables that are retained, the less real memory that is available for the rest of the system.

Solutions

There is no real solution; in fact, there is a trade-off situation that has to be resolved. Someone will have to decide the relative merits of storing shadow page tables and the overhead of CPU cycles in keeping track of redundant shadow page tables after they are no longer active, against the cost of rebuilding shadow page tables that have been dropped.

OTHER SET COMMANDS

The following SET commands are rarely keyed in, but if they are not specified they can cause poor performance on some processors.

SET REMOTE

If the SET REMOTE command is specified in XEDIT profiles, it will often reduce the network message size. The format for the command is:

```
SET REMOTE ON/OFF
```

Response times may suffer for remote terminals if this is not set on because data streams are not optimized for remote transmissions. This is because programs "see" the terminal as local because the logical terminal interface will obscure the characteristics of the device.

SET BMX

The SET BMX command sets up block multiplexor channels rather than selector channels. The command format is:

```
SET BMX ON/OFF
```

A selector channel will transfer data very quickly to and from one single device at a time on a string of I/O devices. If a string of tape drives are on a selector channel, only one will appear to be reading/writing at a time. When block multiplexor channels are used, a block of data for each device is interleaved by the channel. The devices are able to transmit blocks of data at regular intervals. This is illustrated in Figure 6-2. If a string of tape drives are on a block multiplexor channel, they all appear to be working at the same time.

Performance will be degraded if block multiplexing is not turned on. Selector channels are the default except for channel 0, which is always a byte multiplexor channel. (It usually has unit record devices on it.)

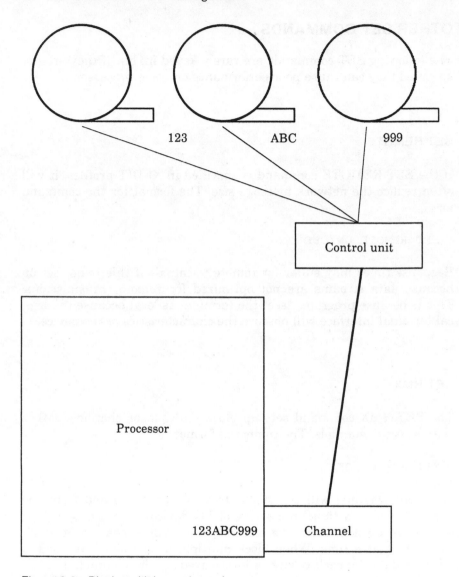

Figure 6-2   Block multiplexor channel.

SET 370E

The SET 370E command improves performance by allowing VM to make use of certain hardware features present on some CPUs. The command format is:

```
SET 370E ON/OFF
```

This feature is useful for MVS and VSE/SP guest systems and is available on 303x, 308x, and 43xx processors. If the feature is not present on the CPU, a CP message will provide this information.

SET AUTOPOLL

The SET AUTOPOLL command is only useful if the guest system is using BTAM. The command format is:

```
SET AUTOPOLL ON/OFF
```

The command reduces the overhead involved when CP has to test whether BTAM CCWs have been dynamically modified. This is not an option on the OPTION directory statement.

SET AFFINITY

The SET AFFINITY command is used in a multiprocessor configuration. The command format is:

```
SET AFFINITY user-id nn
```

This assures that the service virtual machine is dispatched on the processor that has the terminals and FEP (Front End Processor) attached to it.

SET IOASSIST

The SET IOASSIST command is usable on 3090 E processors and higher that are running VM/XA. The command format is:

```
SET IOASSIST guest-id
```

This allows the use of the SIE assist by a preferred guest system.

SET MAXUSER

With XA the SET MAXUSER command can be used to control the load on the system. The format for the command is:

    SET MAXUSER nn

where nn is the number of virtual machines. If a low value is specified it will reduce contention, as fewer virtual machines are able to use the system, and thus will improve performance for those who are using the system. The appropriate value to use will depend on the work that the virtual machines require and the hardware available.

LOCK

The effect of the LOCK command is to retain one or more pages for a specified user-id in real storage. That way the pages are never paged out. The addresses of the critical pages must be given.

Command Format

The command format is:

    LOCK user-id/SYSTEM firstpage lastpage

where firstpage is the start address in storage for the page and lastpage is the last page to be locked. It may be used for more than one virtual machine.

Reasons for Using Command

Page zero is often LOCKed in real storage because it always needs to be in storage when the system is running.

If a CICS system is running under VSE, it is also possible to lock pages containing the CICS nucleus as a way of preventing them from being paged out and thereby improve CICS performance.

If an MVS system is running V=V, it may be useful to lock the whole of its storage. This would prevent double paging.

What Happens

The effect of the command is to prevent the reallocation of specified page frames. These specified pages will remain permanently in real storage. Because no page-out/page-in operations will occur it can lead to a significant improvement in the performance of the user-id concerned.

With an MVS V=V system the pages in the MVS auxiliary storage will be paged into the MVS user area. Because this is already in real storage there is no need for VM to page. Hence double paging is prevented.

Problems Experienced

There are two very obvious problems with the use of a command such as LOCK. The first is similar in nature to that experienced with the SET RESERVE command, which is that the pages in the DPA that are allocated to one user-id cannot be used by all the other virtual machines. This may lead to excessive paging of these other users. Therefore, the improvements for one user may be more than counteracted by the deterioration in the performance of the other users. The second problem is the necessity of knowing exactly the addresses of those pages to be locked.

Solutions

Many sites consider that the best solution to problems posed by the LOCK command is to never use it.

7

I/O

I/O is the name given to the process of moving data and programs in and out of the central electronic complex. Inside the central electronic complex or processor, programs or virtual machines can be executed. The movement of data and programs is controlled by channels or in XA by a subchannel system. Attached to the channels by cable are the control units, and attached to these are one or more devices. The devices may be unit record devices (nowadays represented only by printers), graphic devices (screens), tape drives, or DASD. The majority of active data, databases, and programs are stored on DASD and are regularly backed up to tape. Figure 7-1 illustrates the components of a path from a channel to a DASD.

At many sites I/O is reckoned to be the biggest bottleneck constraining system performance, and, therefore, an understanding of the component parts and the processes involved is very important in terms of performance management and will usually produce the biggest pay-back in terms of tuning.

CHANNEL

A channel is itself a processor that controls I/O to all control units attached to it. Channels are given instructions by Channel Command Words from the main processor. How fast the channel can work limits the speed at which data transfer to and from the control units

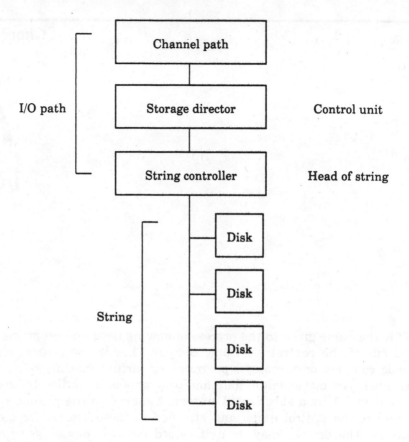

Figure 7-1   Diagram of an I/O path.

can take place. If there is more activity to the devices connected to the channel than the channel can handle, a "channel busy" message will be sent and the I/O operation will be queued.

A channel may be a selector channel, in which case it will select one device and send or receive data from that device only. More commonly a channel will be a multiplexor channel, in which case data to all the attached devices is sent serially. This means that part of the data for device one is sent, then data for device two, then data for device three, and then more data for device one. This is known as time division multiplexing and is illustrated in Figure 6-2. Channels may be block multiplexor channels or byte multiplexor channels. If they are block multiplexor channels, they send and receive data in blocks; if they are byte channels, they send and receive data in bytes. A block is made up of a number of bytes; therefore, a block multiplexor channel is usually faster than a byte multiplexor channel. Channel zero is typically a byte multiplexor channel and has unit record devices (printers, card readers, and card punches) attached to it. With XA systems the concept of a channel has been replaced by a subchannel system which performs the same functions. VM/SP can support up to 16 channels. HPO can support up to 32 channels.

Good performance is usually associated with channel balancing. With VM this means that active files should be spread across a number of disks and a number of channels.

CONTROL UNIT

A control unit controls the flow of data between the devices and the channel. A DASD control unit may receive a command from a channel (e.g., seek, search, read, or write) and execute it on the disk. The controller tells the channels the result of executing the command.

If a multiported controller is used, there is a hierarchy of interrupt servicing in the case of two processors trying to communicate with it at the same time. The slower CPU should be placed on the A interface. If the fastest processor is placed on the A interface, the controller will be satisfying its requests for service and rarely get a chance to service requests via the B interface; therefore, the slower processor will appear to be running very slowly.

DISK

A disk is basically a central spindle with a number of platters placed one above the other attached to the spindle. This is illustrated in Figure 7-2. There are two families of disks. There are CKD (Count Key Data) disks in which the area covered by a single head without the head moving during a single rotation of the platter and central spindle is defined as a track. The area covered by all the heads without the heads moving during a single rotation of all the platters and central spindle is defined as a cylinder. As the head moves toward the central spindle, the area that is covered by a single rotation is decreased. However, a track on the outside of a platter holds the same amount of data as a track near the middle of the platter because the data is stored more densely nearer the center. With CKD disks, each data block is preceded by a count area and an optional key area. This is shown in Figure 7-3. Data in the count area can be

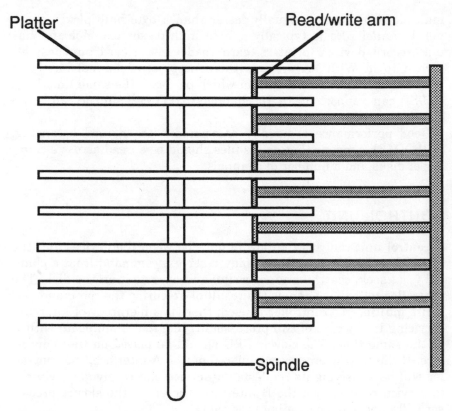

Figure 7-2   Diagram of a DASD.

used to ensure that the disk is accessing the correct block of data. Data blocks can be variable in length. There is always a gap between the count, key, and data areas. The more blocks that are stored, the more gaps there will be and the more space that will be wasted. Cylinder 0 contains the allocation records for the device. This is used during I/O processing to locate mini-disks. It also contains information regarding the use of the mini-disk, i.e., paging, spooling, dump, etc. 3380 disks have 15 tracks to a cylinder, and there are 885 (or multiples thereof) cylinders on a 3380.

The other family of disks are FBA (Fixed Block Architecture) disks. These are divided up into fixed size sectors and offer advantages to the user in not having to worry about block sizes. All disk blocks are 512 bytes in size, and a 3370 disk can store 558,000 of them. FBA disks are not supported by XA.

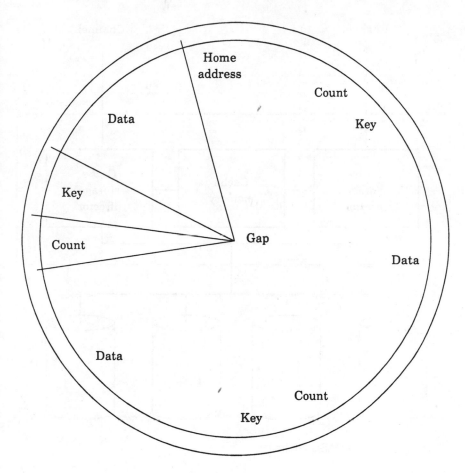

Figure 7-3   Count key data format.

The read/write heads are grouped together to form a Head Disk Assembly (HDA) unit. This moves across the platters from one cylinder to another. This movement is called a seek.

All current disk models rotate at 3600 revolutions per minute.

CACHE

Disk cache storage was conceived as a way to improve effective disk performance, thereby removing disk bottleneck problems. Cache is a high speed buffer, which can be located in DASD controllers (the

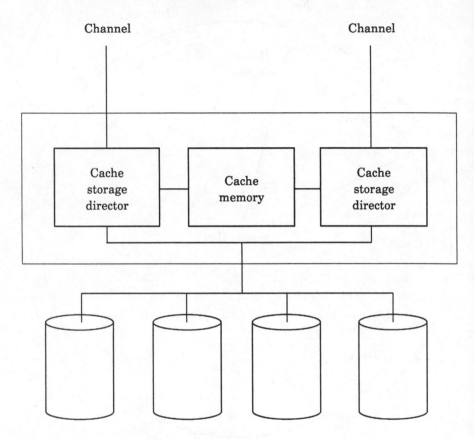

Figure 7-4   Cache DASD controller.

3880 models and above). The cache controllers contain what are called storage directors that control access to DASD. This is illustrated in Figure 7-4. Cache memory is similar to that used in main storage. It contains a directory that can be scanned by the storage directors to see if the record is already in cache and a storage area that can contain the records. Accessing files in cache is much faster than having to access files on disk.

To access a file in cache a CCW (Channel Command Word) is passed to a channel, which tells the controller to perform the I/O. The storage director will search the cache directory to see if the track containing the record is already in cache. If it is, the file is transferred to the channel. If the file is not in cache, the storage director will access the file on disk and put a copy in cache memory and pass a copy to the channel. A heavily used track will stay in cache, which makes its access time very fast. Updated records are written to the disk and not stored in cache.

If a record about to be read is located in the cache, the overall device response time is reduced dramatically. The access time is practically instantaneous and the transfer of data can proceed at the maximum rate for the channel. Cache memory sizes that are currently available range from 8 MB to 64 MB, depending on the vendor and the control unit model.

The higher the percentage of requests satisfied from the cache, the greater the performance improvement. Cache control units only benefit from high read hit ratios, as writes must always be directed to the DASD volume for data integrity purposes. Therefore, for writes, a Device End interrupt is not posted until the data is written successfully to disk, which elongates the I/O response times for the write.

The higher the percentage of I/O requests satisfied by the cache (hit ratio), the better, or more consistent, the performance. Devices that do not meet these characteristics can actually degrade performance.

Cached data must have the following three attributes for caching to be effective:

• High I/O rates
• Locality of reference
• High read to write ratio

Cache cannot be used by VM/SP systems.

SOLID STATE DEVICES

Solid state devices are DASD with very fast I/O times. They can achieve this because they use semi-conductor memory and have no moving parts; therefore, there is no time lost during seek activity or rotational delay. However, they do not release the host channel to locate a record, and this results in erratic response times for non-cache DASD. The 0.3 msec access time results in, typically, 2–4 msec I/O response times, depending on the blocksize. Between 300 and 400 I/O requests per second per I/O path are commonly attainable. Because there is no delay due to the RPS (Rotational Position Sensing) factor of rotating DASD and any data staging overhead of cached DASD, channel utilization values in excess of 70 percent busy can be achieved before any significant channel queuing occurs.

Though not a requirement, high-performance disks usually reside on dedicated channels.

EXPANDED STORAGE

In some of the more modern processors the storage can be divided into two parts. The part used for real storage is called central storage. The rest is called expanded storage. This expanded storage can be used for paging and for caching mini-disk directories. All paging addresses are resolved at the page level in expanded storage rather than at the segment level. Paging in and out of expanded storage is much faster than to disk, although the activity is synchronous, which means that all activity is stopped until the page transfer is complete. The use of expanded storage saves disk space and reduces the amount of I/O that has to be performed. It is a way of improving performance.

Guest operating systems can use part of expanded storage to improve their performance. It can also be used by CMS, but only 4K formatted mini-disks are eligible for caching in expanded storage.

PATH

A path is defined as the route that can be taken by a message from a channel or subchannel through a control unit to a device (or head of string and device) or from a device via a control unit to a channel or subchannel. Note that a string controller can be directly connected to a channel or to a storage director.

DYNAMIC PATH SELECTION

With XA, there is a facility for the subchannel system to dynamically try to find a path to a device. If one path is busy, it will try any available alternatives.

DYNAMIC PATH RECONNECT

With XA, data from a device does not have to return to the channel along the same path as the original request for the data reached the disk. If alternative paths are available, the data will be transmitted back to the subchannel using that path.

IOCP

The Input Output Configuration Program is located in the processor controller. It contains a definition of the I/O devices and paths that are connected to the processor. It plays an important role with XA. If a path or a device is not configured in the IOCP, the device or path cannot be used. The IoCP is created by an IOCPgen.

MINI-DISKS

A real disk may be formatted into mini-disks. These mini-disks can be allocated to virtual machines. Each virtual machine will have the mini-disks available to it defined in the directory entry for that user. For example, a CMS user will typically have a mini-disk at address 191 with a letter designation of A. This mini-disk will usually contain the EXECs and data files of that CMS user. Also allocated are an S disk (the system disk), a D disk, and a Y disk. The S and the Y disks are maintained by the MAINT user-id, and all CMS users are LINKed to them. A directory at the front of each mini-disk contains pointers to all the files on the mini-disk.

When a user logs on there will be control blocks associated with these mini-disks which are stored in the Free Storage Area (FSA). When a user wishes to access a mini-disk, the control blocks are used to translate the virtual address into a real address so that the request for access can go to the correct real disk.

Temporary Mini-Disks

A user can allocate temporary mini-disks at any time. A temporary mini-disk can be used as a temporary file. TDSK space is created using the CP FORMAT command, and the space for temporary mini-disks is taken from that area.

To allocate temporary disk space a user enters:

```
CP DEFINE T3380 195 6
FORMAT 195 F
```

```
YES
VMP009
```

where

195	=	virtual addres
6	=	number of cylinders to be allocated
F	=	the filemode to be used
VMP009	=	the volser of the disk

Accessing Mini-Disks

Users often need to access mini-disks belonging to other users, for example, MAINT, in order to make a copy of a particular file. A user must LINK to a user's disk before accessing it. To free up a disk it must be released and detached. An example of the sequence of commands is given below:

```
LINK altuser 191 199 R
ACCESS 199 T
  LIST * * T
  COPYFILE fn ft T = = A
REL T
DET 199
```

where

altuser	=	another virtual machine
191	=	the virtual address of the required mini-disk
199	=	the virtual address it will be for the user
R	=	read-only access
T	=	filemode for the user

CHANNEL COMMAND WORD

A Channel Command Word (CCW) is a doubleword (i.e., 8 bytes). One or more CCWs can be used to tell the channel what activity to perform. Some typical CCWs are:

- Seek
- Set Sector
- Search
- TIC (Transfer in Channel)
- Read Count Key Data
- Read Sector

Seek

Seek instructs the actuator to move to the correct cylinder. Having initiated this process, the channel and control unit are released and can be used for other devices.

Set Sector

Set sector identifies an angular displacement from Record 0. When the read/write heads are over that sector, the channel and control unit should be reconnected to the device. If the reconnection cannot be made because the channel or control unit is busy, the disk will spin through 360 degrees before another attempt is made to reconnect. This process is called Rotational Position Sensing (RPS) and is installed on all modern disks. If the device is a 3380 and Dynamic Path Reconnection can be used (VM/XA environments only), both possible routes from the disk will be checked for reconnection.

Search

Search instructs the channel, control unit, and device to look for a particular record by address. This address will be 5 bytes in length and will contain a hexadecimal address of the form CCCCHHHHRR, where CCCC is the cylinder number, HHHH is the track number within the cylinder, and RR is the record number on the track.

TIC (Transfer In Channel)

TIC is a branch instruction in a channel program. If the preceding search is successful, it will be bypassed. If not, the TIC branches back to the *search* and it is repeated.

Read Count Key Data

Read count key data reads the count of the record, any key recorded, and the data into main storage.

Read Sector

Read sector reads the sector number of the record just read into storage for use by the next channel program.

Write Channel Program

A write channel program is similar to a read. However, there are two forms of DASD write. It is possible to write a new record or to update a record in place. The first form is called format write and is implemented as a write count, key, and data instruction. When the data record has been written, the device disconnects from the channel but continues to write binary zeros on the rest of the track, thus invalidating any previous records. The second form is implemented as a write data or write key and data. Here, the data length of the key and record may not change, and hence the remainder of the track is not overwritten. The first form is typically used by sequential output processing, the second is used by any update-in-place processing whether sequential, direct, or keyed. Note that one implication of this is that all direct or keyed files must be sequentially loaded with real or dummy records before any nonsequential use is made of them.

I/O SEQUENCE OF EVENTS

The sequence of events that occurs in an I/O operation (3380 device) is composed of software and hardware events. They can be summarized as:

* Queue time
      Wait for device
      Wait for path
* Seeking
      Seek

Latency
RPS reconnect delay
* Connect time
Search
Data transfer
* Protocol

Queue Time

Wait for Device   A virtual machine must wait for a device if that device is being used by another virtual machine on the same system. The only tuning that can be done to reduce the wait time is to decrease the device busy time.

Wait for Path   Once the I/O operation is successfully initiated, the I/O must still wait in the channel subsystem until a path to the device becomes available. All components of the path (i.e., channel, control unit, head of string, and internal data path) must be free.

If the path is available, the system can attempt to access the device, unless it is kept busy by another system (shared DASD).

Seeking

Seek   When the device and the path are free, the system can start the I/O operation. The I/O operation is usually started with a seek command initiated by the control unit. This ignores the time it takes to process the seek CCW and the set sector CCW.

Once the device receives the seek information, the channel, control unit, and string controller are released and can process other I/O requests. The time required to move the arm to the cylinder and to select the correct track head is referred to as seek time. Seek times for the 3380 device are:

* Minimum—3 msec
* Average—16 msec
* Maximum—30 msec

Typically about 30 percent of DASD I/O requests result in non-zero seeks. The average time for an I/O request can be calculated as 16 msec × 0.33 = 5.3 msec. Because seeking activity depends on the reference pattern for that disk, the time taken can be reduced by controlling the placement of files.

Latency It is impossible to predict the current position of a rotating disk relative to the position of the required sector. On average, half a rotation, the so-called latency, must elapse before the correct sector position is reached.

RPS Reconnect Delay Once the correct sector position is reached, the device will try to reconnect to the path. There is very little time to do this (because the disk is spinning at 3600 rpm), and if the attempt is unsuccessful the device (actuator) must try again during the next revolution. If this happens, an RPS delay of one full revolution (16.7 msec) occurs. The RPS reconnect delay is clearly a function of the path being busy because of the activity of other actuators on the same path. With SP and HPO the data must return down the channel that initiated the I/O operation. As channel utilizations increase, the chance of the channel being busy increases exponentially. With XA any device path can be used for reconnection. Thus, the probability of finding an available path is much higher under XA; consequently, the impact of RPS misses is diminished. RPS misses are indicated by high service times being revealed by a monitor. RPS delay due to path contention is a function of the path being busy at various times during the I/O operation. Therefore, tuning to reduce this delay is done by decreasing path busy time.

Connect Time

Search Data cannot be read or written until the requested record location has been verified using a search ID or search on KEY command. The search time is usually very short (1 msec).

Data Transfer When the correct block (record) is found, data transfer can begin at device speed. The time taken for the data transfer can be calculated by dividing the block size by the data transfer speed of the device (e.g., 4K block divided by 3MB/sec for the 3380 yields 1.36 msec).

Protocol

In the control unit (e.g., 3880), the initiation and completion of each command requires a finite amount of time. This processing results in the path being busy because the control unit is part of the path to the device. A further part of the processing overlaps with device activity. The value of the protocol time is dependent on the 3880 microcode level and is therefore variable (±1.6 msec).

PATH SELECTION

If there are two paths available to access a bank of disks, VM does not perform path rotation, but will always attempt to start the I/O on the primary path. If a busy condition is encountered, it will try the alternate path.

The latest machines (e.g., 3080s and 3090s) using the SIOF instruction always queue in the channel. The advantage of this is that it relieves CP of the work required to handle busy conditions and requeuing the I/O. The disadvantage is that CP never sees a busy condition and, therefore, never invokes its alternate path logic. The result is that all I/O goes down the primary path.

One way of reducing this problem, and thereby improving performance, is to alternate the definition of which is the primary path. This is done in the DMKRIO macro. An example is given below:

```
RDEVICE ADDRESS=120,DEVTYPE=3350,ALTCU=220
RDEVICE ADDRESS=122,DEVTYPE=3350,ALTCU=220

RDEVICE ADDRESS=221,DEVTYPE=3350,ALTCU=120
RDEVICE ADDRESS=223,DEVTYPE=3350,ALTCU=120
```

or

```
RDEVICE ADDRESS=(120,4),DEVTYPE=3350,ALTCU=220
RDEVICE ADDRESS=(224,4),DEVTYPE=3350,ALTCU=120
```

SP and HPO systems redrive the I/O via the alternate channel (ALTCH in DMKRIO), if present, before using the alternate control unit (ALTCU in DMKRIO). If there is only one control unit on the channel it is likely to still be busy, and the I/O will again fail.

With HPO another solution to the problem is to make a modification to the DMKIOQ macro (DMKIOS for HPO release 3 users) which can be used to make CP flip-flop between channels. This is given below:

```
./ * FLIP-FLOP PATHS TO BALANCE CHANNELS TO REDUCE
./ * QUEUEING IN 3083 CHANNELS
./ I 18670000  18670010  10        (for DMKIOS on HPO 3.0)
./ I 04300000  04300010  10        (for DMKIOQ on HPO 3.4)
         NC     RDEVCUB,RDEVCUB     IF NO ALTERNATE CU
         BZ     NOFLIP              DO NOT FLIP-FLOP
         TM     RDEVPTHS,RDEVAOF    NO FLIP-FLOP
         BO     NOFLIP              IF
         TM     RDEVPTHS,REDVBOF    EITHER CU
         BO     NOFLIP              HAS ALL PATHS OFFLINE
         TM     RDEVOFF,X'FF'       NO FLIP-FLOP IF PATH
         BNZ    NOFLIP              OFFLINE AT THE MOMENT
         L      R0,RDEVCUB          FLIP-FLOP PATHS TO BALANCE
         MVC    RDEVCUB,RDEVCUA     3083 CHANNELS, SINCE
         ST     R0,RDEVCUA          THEY WILL Q INTERNALLY
*               FLIP-FLOP OFFLINE   SWITCHES FOR CONTROL UNITS
         PACK   RDEVPTHS,RDEVPTHS   REVERSE BYTE
NOFLIP   EQU    *
```

If any site with SLU406 or above plans to use this fix, it should be applied after label FXPTH rather than 04300000.

VM/XA does not suffer from the lack of path rotation. Rotation is performed automatically by the channel subsystem rather than VM/XA itself. The IOCP must accurately match the hardware configuration or channels, etc., may not be used. Each device must be defined by only one IODEVICE macro.

XA uses a never-ending channel program (suspend resume). The effect of this is that paging packs will appear to be around 95 percent busy. This value is not a true indicator and can be confusing especially when looking at monitor reports.

START I/O

Older processors and older operating systems used the Start I/O (SIO) instruction. Newer operating systems use the Start I/O Fast release (SIOF) instruction.

An I/O request cannot be started if a device, control unit, or channel are busy. If an alternative path is available, this will be used to try to start the I/O. If all paths are busy, the I/O request is queued at the appropriate level in the I/O subsystem. As soon as that level becomes available, CP will try to perform the oldest I/O in the queue.

When a guest issues a Start I/O (SIO) instruction its execution is suspended until the corresponding real SIO can be performed; i.e., it is put in an IOWAIT state. This stops it running or dispatching any partitions. CP will queue the I/O until the path is free and then start the I/O. If a channel or control unit busy condition is received, CP will requeue the I/O and retry later. When VM has finally successfully issued the I/O, it will reflect the appropriate condition code to the guest and start running the guest again.

Example condition codes include:

• Successful
• Device busy
• Device not operational

The guest must remain suspended until CP knows which condition code to present to it.

If the guest uses the SIOF instruction, the guest can be redispatched immediately because the definition of the SIOF instruction allows for deferred condition codes to be presented later if the I/O is not successfully initiated. The use of SIOF does require additional programming support.

If the guest is run on an old processor that does not implement the SIOF instruction, it will be treated as an SIO. All current versions of MVS, VSE, and VM use the SIOF instruction. This reduces IOWAITs and so improves performance.

Some processors have an SIOFQing facility available. Although it is sometimes recommended that this be turned off, in general, it is usually beneficial to utilize the facility.

CP schedules most I/O using a FIFO algorithm. The exception to this rule is paging—due to its importance in terms of performance. Paging I/O is handled in preference to normal I/O activity.

CMS virtual machines use the DIAGNOSE instruction interface to perform most of their I/O. Because this is synchronous, the virtual machine will be suspended until the I/O operation completes.

RESOURCE CONSUMPTION

I/O simulation consumes resources. I/O commands must be translated from virtual to real addresses, and I/O buffers from virtual to real storage addresses. I/Os to mini-disks require virtual to real cylinder address translation. With XA, it must also convert a 370 SIO command to an XA SSCH (Start SubCHannel) command.

An I/O request from a virtual machine will use up CPU cycles and storage when it is interpreted. CP has to translate the channel program so that it references the correct pages, accommodates mini-disk relocation, and honors read-only device status. A copy of the channel program is made by CP, and the addresses and control words are relocated appropriately.

Reducing the CP overhead by reducing the number of I/Os makes more of the CP available for productive work. Dedicated DASDs reduce the amount of translation work.

SPOOLING

The use of the spool can be a major cause of I/O resource consumption. The spool is formated into 4K pages and is used to store print files, reader files, and punch files.

Both spooling and paging transfer data in units of 4K. The spooling subsystem uses the paging subsystem to perform all its I/O. The spooling manager uses the same CCPD designation when writing the page-out. With SP and HPO there are no separate counters, and so it is impossible to distinguish I/O for paging from I/O for spooling. The results from the IND PAG command always include spool paging, and so high values may not mean high amounts of paging but may indicate high amounts of spooling. With XA there are four counters that can be used to separate spooling activities from paging activities. These are PLSPIOPR, PLSPIOPW, PLSPIOSR, PLSPIOSW.

PAGE and spool areas can be kept separate using format/allocate PAGE. If this is done, then separate information about spooling and paging can be obtained.

Paging and spooling always take precedence over other I/Os. If S and Y disks are placed on the same packs as either paging or spooling, the response to CMS users will be greatly inhibited.

Paging will spill into spool (TEMP) space if there is not enough of it. This will prevent the system from crashing. Spool files will not overflow into paging areas.

Performance problems can occur if the spool area (specified as TEMP during system set up) is allowed to fill up. Users will receive "intervention required" messages on virtual unit record output devices. More importantly, accounting and monitoring data may be lost. It is always a good idea to purge unwanted spool files on a regular basis.

With SP, problems occur with the spool area filling up because users sometimes treat it as a mini-disk overflow area. It also degrades performance because of the resulting large numbers of SFBLOKs in the FSA. Another problem occurs should a checkpoint (CKPT) or force start be required. Verifying spool chains can make the process take a long time. A checkpoint start of VM may take up to 15 minutes while spool file chains are validated.

With HPO release 5 and above, the system can support up to 9900 spool files per user. The total number of spool files supported is specified with the DMKSYS SYSSPL option on the SYSRES macro. However, there is also a limitation enforced by the size of the checkpoint area. With HPO release 5, reader SFBLOKs are stored in the DPA and the performance of both checkpoint and force starts is improved with the use of overlapping I/O.

With XA, spooling is used for the following:

• Virtual machine spooling
• CP monitoring data
• Dumps
• DCSSs and NSSs
• Printer FCBs and UCBs
• User class override file

The performance benefit associated with this is that DCSS and FCRs can be introduced without requiring an IPL.

The best performance can be achieved if enough space is made available and spread across as many DASDs as possible.

XA can support up to 9999 files per user, although the total number of spool files for an individual user can be limited by the SPOOL-

FILE MAXSPOOL directory entry. The total number of spool files supported may be restricted by the size of the checkpoint start area. It is worth remembering that one 3380 cylinder can support almost 154,000 spool files.

If no user mini-disks are placed on disks with spool files, the disks will not need to be backed up with the nightly back-ups. This can save time. However, if things are arranged in this way it is a good idea to, occasionally, perform SPTAPE back-ups of the spool files.

MONITORS

It can be useful to monitor certain areas associated with I/O. These include:

- Number of I/O operations
- Total of I/O queue time
- Total device service time
- Total seek time
- Total latency time
- Total connected time
- Total RPS delay time

An I/O bottleneck is seen as large I/O wait values and correspondingly low CPU utilization levels.

The IND I/O and IND LOAD commands can reveal useful information about I/O. The IND I/O command will show which users are waiting for I/O operations to start or complete and which devices they are waiting for. If this command is entered repeatedly, it can show up troublespots. The IND LOAD will show which users are waiting for an I/O operation to start and which are waiting for it to finish.

One way of identifying I/O problems is to enter Q IOWAIT from the MAINT virtual machine. This will show which virtual machines are waiting for an I/O operation to complete. This command will take a snapshot of the system and will need to be repeated to get a true picture. If 25 percent or more of the logged on users are waiting, this indicates a problem. If one user-id consistently shows up as waiting, it indicates the source of the problem.

VMMAP Indicators

VMMAP's PAGEWAIT and IOWAIT variables are good indicators of problems. Any upward trend in the values from these figures indicates a growing problem.

A full description of how some of the displayed results are obtained is given below.

The number of I/O operations per path is estimated from the path usage sample associated with each I/O event in the head movement record.

The queue time by path is found by taking the average queue time for the device multiplied by the I/O count for the path.

Device service time by path is the number of path-busy samples divided by the total samples and multiplied by the duration of the observation period. For XA, device service time is the sum of the hardware-measured connected and disconnected times.

Seek time by path is the average seek time for the device multiplied by the I/O count for the path. The average seek time for the device is calculated from the sequence of cylinder addresses for each device in the head movement record. This sequence can be used to estimate the number of nonsequential seek requests and uses seek-timing tables to convert the number of cylinders traversed into seek time.

Latency by path is the average latency for the device multiplied by the I/O count for the path.

Connected time by path is the average connected time for the device times the I/O count for the path.

RPS delay time by path is calculated by subtracting seek time, latency, and connected time (all by path) from device service time by path.

A STRATEGY FOR PERFORMANCE MANAGEMENT

There are two suggested strategies to optimize DASD performance: separation and dedication, or spreading the load. Although the first case is often made by IBM, it is rarely achievable. The object of the second approach is to ensure that channels, control units, and string access paths are as evenly loaded as possible, and this can be achieved. In practice, the objective has been achieved when channels and control units are either evenly balanced, + or − 5 percent, or are less than 20 percent busy. In fact, no channel, control unit, or device is ever 20 percent busy—it is either 100 percent or 0 percent busy.

PERFORMANCE VERSUS CAPACITY

Large installations usually place a multiplicity of demands on their storage subsystems, e.g., reliability, performance, capacity, function, and flexibility. These demands may, from time to time, conflict. Achieving acceptable performance from a device while utilizing a reasonable amount of its storage capacity is a conflict often resolved by compromise. In many large-system environments, 90 percent of performance problems are related to I/O performance. Studies have shown that in most large systems, 60 percent of the I/Os are going to only 1 percent of the data. Making that 1 percent more available without decreasing efficiency is part of the solution in balancing performance and capacity requirements.

CHANNEL AND CONTROL UNIT LOADINGS

For DASD devices, channel and control unit loadings should not exceed 30 percent and preferably should be lower than that. If channels are dedicated to 3380s with Dynamic Path Reconnect, the value may be increased to around 40 percent for the equivalent performance. However, it is usually thought better to take the improvement in performance than to risk overloading the channels.

If a very well-tuned cache controller is installed, higher rates may be sustained safely. If solid state devices are used, values up to 70 percent channel busy are acceptable.

DASD PERFORMANCE

Seek, latency, data transfer, and RPS miss are the major response components of a DASD I/O, and all can vary as the device and I/O path get busier. Unlike high-performance DASD where the RPS factor is zero, every RPS miss adds another 16.7 msec to DASD I/O response time. As path busy approaches 35 percent, queuing theory indicates that one full DASD revolution of 16.7 msec (at 3600 rpm)

Table 7-1   Performance comparison.

	Channel busy Max percent	I/O rate (4K)/sec	Initial service time (msec)
High-performance DASD	70–75	700–800	1–3
Cache DASD	50–60	200–300	5–20
DASD	35–45	90–100	20–50

will occur for every successful I/O. Dual ported I/O was introduced in the 1970s and significantly helped the RPS misses issue. In addition to dual port, dynamic path reconnect also helps reduce RPS miss by allowing the I/O operations from the device to reconnect to the host via a path other than the one on which it was initiated. This is available with VM/XA. Table 7-1 illustrates performance comparisons between high-performance DASD, cache DASD, and noncache DASD subsystems.

When looking at DASD performance it is worth considering the access density or the I/O rate/sec/Gbyte of storage. This index has declined steadily since 1970. On a per unit storage basis, the unit of storage has less performance capability with each new device that is introduced. Performance per DASD actuator has not kept up with the increased capacity per actuator, and this has reduced the I/O capabilities of the device per unit of storage.

Traditionally, seek times and RPS delays are likely to be the largest single factors within I/O service time, but seek times have been greatly reduced on more recent disk devices. The usual solution to seek problems is to reorganize the placement of files and mini-disks; unfortunately, with the latest disks, the time required to establish seek patterns and reorganize mini-disks will often not be worthwhile.

Having found the bottlenecked drives, they must be identified on the (up-to-date) configuration diagram. It may well be that they are located within the same string. Detailed path analysis (using the path reports) can be used to find the contending paths that caused these drives to be delayed. The solution to contention is isolation, giving the applications that require responsiveness the preferred paths that they need.

SAVING DISK SPACE

It is impossible to tune a system if there is so little spare capacity on a disk that any file shifting results in the whole pack having to be reorganized. Extra DASD will need to be purchased or the space used reduced.

Until the Shared File System (SFS) becomes widely used, real disks will continue to be formatted into mini-disks. The space allocated to each mini-disk could be reduced or the need for extra mini-disks for each user postponed if redundant information is eliminated. This is a standard means of reducing the amount of resources required to store a given quantity of data. There are a variety of compression algorithms available that can take a logical or physical unit of data (i.e., a record or a block) and make it smaller by, for example, replacing runs of identical bytes with shorter control indicator fields. Of course, the data must be expanded back to its exact original form before the user is allowed to see it again.

FILE PLACEMENT AND PERFORMANCE

Ideal I/O performance could be achieved by placing one file in each mini-disk, one mini-disk per real disk, one real disk per string, one string per control unit, and one control unit per channel. This is almost never achieved and a compromise between cost and performance is the norm.

The speed with which data on disk can be accessed varies significantly with the location of that data. Of major importance is the device type; for example, data can usually be accessed more quickly on a solid-state storage device than on a dual-density 3350. Within a group of like devices, the particular device chosen can also have a significant influence on performance. A device that is currently taking 20 I/O operations per second is probably going to deliver worse performance than one that is averaging 3 per second. However, a device's I/O rate may vary significantly during different times of the day. Finally, the specific location chosen on a volume is usually important. If there are other active files on the volume, placement near those files will tend to reduce seek activity (assuming it is a seeking device). Fixed-head areas on certain disks require special treatment as they are not subject to seek phenomena.

APPLICATIONS

When tuning a system, performance improvements can often result from improving the way an application deals with I/O. Some suggested ways to improve I/O performance include:

- An increase in the block size—this should reduce the amount of I/O activity and should enhance performance.
- A complete redesign of the application.
- A redesign of the data structure within the application.

The use of additional main storage might reduce the amount of I/O but may increase the amount of paging.

NEW HARDWARE

New hardware may be required if queues persist for devices, control units, or channels. However, newer disks with fewer access arms for more data do tend to degrade throughput. Also, the use of alternate paths tends to improve availability but does not usually offer any performance gains.

Improvements can be made by dedicating resources to large or highly active virtual machines. If several users are isolated so that the only contention they experience is between themselves, this can be a useful way to use additional hardware.

The use of cache controllers can improve I/O performance provided that appropriate files are cached.

USEFUL SET COMMANDS

The following SET commands can be used to help improve I/O performance (full details are given in Chapter 6):

SP commands

    SET SRM APAGES
    SET SRM MAXWSS
    SET PAGING

HPO commands

SET MINWS
SET SRM MAXPP
SET SRM PREPAGE
SET SRM SWPQTIME

XA commands

SET IOASSIST
SET MAXUSER
SET QUICKDSP
SET SHARE ABS/REL
SET SRM LDBUF
SET SRM STORBUF
SET SRM DSPBUF

HINTS AND TIPS

- If heavily used software is placed on a separate disk, there are two advantages. There is an improvement in performance. It is also possible to audit the use of that software. This is done by utilizing the VM accounting data.
- It is worth considering duplicating disks if the number of active users to them exceeds 50. An example would be the CMS S disk. The duplicate should be from a DDR back-up so that all copies use the same shared S-STATs. The duplicate copy should be put on a different disk pack to avoid contention. For the CMS Y disk it must have the same Y-stats. If the mini-disks are cached, then it is often not worth duplicating them, provided that a high number of users are accessing them. Because the files will be continuously accessed they will stay in cache storage and, thus, better performance will be achieved. With SP release 5, the more heavily used EXECs can be placed in shared segments. This relieves the strain on the Y disk and improves access times to those EXECs.
- Heavily used mini-disks (for example the CMS S and Y disks) can have their access times reduced if the files on them are placed in order. The order used should be a frequency of use order, with the most heavily used file first. Although the exercise may be time

consuming, the benefits from it are considerable. It is worthwhile doing it on a new disk so that the files are not fragmented—if this is possible.

- Allocating multiple mini-disks can be done using the directory. However, this is tedious and there is a software aid on the Waterloo tapes which will automate the procedure. The program is called "IPLER".

- Heavily used mini-disks will yield better performance if they are placed near the center of the pack and placed next to each other. This reduces the amount of head movement required to access them. It is also recommended that the minimum number of heavily used mini-disks possible are placed on any one pack.

- The best performance can be achieved if the busiest DASD volumes are placed at the end of a string. When a volume on a string is ready to be serviced, a flag is set at the volume. These flags are ORed together at the head of string. When it detects a service request flag, the head of string controller starts a sequential search of the string, checking to see which one requires service. When a flag is found, the controller services the volume and resets the flag. The controller will then return to the beginning. If the service request flag is still set, it begins the search again. If a heavily used pack is placed at the beginning of string, it will tend to hog the service cycles and so lock out the trailing volumes which will be waiting for service. If less heavily used volumes are placed at the start of the string, they will be serviced more quickly and will be out of the path when the second scan is done.

- The 3380s A and D models were highly thought of because of the amount of data that they could store. However, there is only one path available for the whole string. As the disks get busier, the likelihood of a busy head of string occurring increases. It is recommended that only one box (i.e., four addresses) on a string be used, and that a maximum of three be used.

- With model Es, Js, and Ks there are four paths to service a maximum of 16 volumes on each string. Busy volumes should always be placed at the end of each substring, otherwise they will lock-out the less busy volumes.

- Because 3380 models A04, AA04, and AD04 have only one path to service up to 16 volumes, it is imperative that volumes be placed in the correct order in the string.

- With 3380 models AE04, AJ04, and AK04 there are four paths to each unit servicing four units in the string. Heavily used volumes should be placed at the end of the string.

- Heavily used strings should be placed lower on controllers, and heavily used controllers should be placed further down channels for similar reasons.
- Also, virtual addresses should be allocated in a similar way because of the way that RDEVBLOKs are processed. Therefore, terminals should be on lower addresses than tape drives.
- An analysis of seek activity on a DASD can indicate highly used areas. A map of the allocated areas of the volume will show which virtual machines are responsible for activity against each area. Examination of disk access analysis should be carried out at different times of the day because there may be a wide variation in the pattern of access, and there is no point tuning for only one of several different access patterns.
- The SAVEFD command can be used to make file directories of common mini-disks shared. This saves on I/O and storage.
- It is never a good idea to put terminals on the same channels as paging packs. The service to the terminals will have to wait until disk I/O is complete.
- The heavy use of TDISKs can impact on I/O performance. Formatting is I/O intensive and can slow down other I/O activity.
- I/O activity needs to be balanced across devices, control units, and channels.
- System mini-disks should not be all put on one actuator; the load should be spread.
- Actuators should be dedicated to PROFS DASD; i.e., they should not be shared with active data.
- The RECFM V parameter saves disk space, but RECFM F is faster.
- CMS mini-disks should be formatted using a block size of 4K.
- All the items on DASD should be cached, not just some. If some items are not cached, I/O takes place at normal DASD speed for that item. When I/O completes cache speed, I/O can take place. If only some items are cached, it loses all the advantages of caching.
- Page and data contention on the same channel should be avoided.
- A reduction in the number of I/Os carried out will improve overall performance.
- Dedicating DASD reduces the amount of translation work required by CP.
- If 3380s are not formatted into 4K blocks, a lot of space is wasted by the size of Inter-Block Gaps (IBG). No other number divides so exactly into the track size of a 3380 as 4K blocks do.

- The only reason for not using a 4K block size would be for mini-disks that contain very, very small files.
- CMS release 5, which has read ahead, will get 2 blocks during an I/O operation rather than just one. If 4K blocks are used, this means that 8K will be transferred.

8

Networks

The number of VM users who are working from a terminal connected to a network rather than from a local terminal is increasing all the time, and so the performance of the network is an important component in their perception of the performance of the system as a whole. This makes it an important component of performance management. If members of the public come into contact with a terminal, they tend to perceive network performance as an indication of company performance.

With the growth in distributed data processing, the performance of the network becomes even more important as the user may be working at a great distance from the main processor and connected via a number of subsidiary processing elements.

A communications network can be defined as a set of intelligent devices connected, using a discrete pattern of telecommunications media, allowing communication between any two parts of it without requiring a direct link between those parts.

PERFORMANCE CRITERIA

The ideal objective for the performance of a system is obviously 100 percent availability and instant response. However, this is not possible.

Good network performance can be considered as the immediate transmission of messages from terminals to the software inside the processor and the transmission of messages from software inside the processor to its display on the terminal.

There are three key factors in network performance. They are:

• The availability of the service
• The recoverability of the service
• The quality of the available service

The quality of the service can be considered to be:

• The speed of message delivery
• The number of errors
• The throughput
• The response times

NETWORK PLANNING

When planning a network, or changes to a network, it is necessary to consider four criteria, which are interdependent. They are:

• Cost
• Throughput
• Response
• Reliability

A network should be designed to cater to a minimum number of transactions giving a maximum response time for a certain cost. By varying each of these factors its effect on the others can be seen. Reliability, the fourth variable, has a major impact on cost only, but, if poor, the effect on overall throughput can be considerable.

A working definition of good network performance would be that the original design objects of the network are being met. This means that budgets are not exceeded, the required availability is being provided, and response times satisfy the original throughput objective.

NETWORK COMPONENTS

The performance of the network can be considered in terms of its hardware and software components.

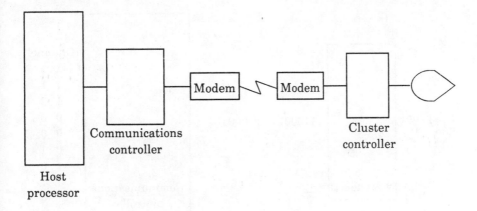

Figure 8-1   Hardware components of a network.

Hardware Components

The main hardware components in a network are:

* Host processor
* Communications controller
* Modem
* Telecommunications network
* Cluster controller
* Terminal

These components are illustrated in Figure 8-1.

Added to these may be various associated switching and multiplexing devices. There must be a number of cables and connectors to complete the link from terminal to host and though these are unlikely to fail on their own, they are very susceptible to a carelessly wielded screwdriver or just wear and tear.

Host Processor The host processor will be running the software, i.e., VM and probably RSCS and VTAM under GCS. The processor will connect to the communications controller through a cable attached to a channel or channel path.

Communications Controller The communications controller (e.g., IBM 3725) is programmable and can perform much of the work required to run the network, thus freeing the processor from this

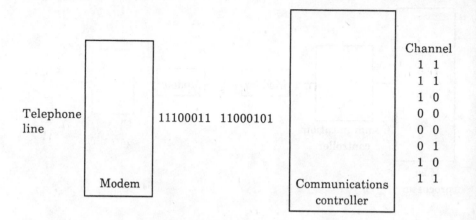

Conversion from serial by bit, serial by character to parallel by bit, serial by character and vice versa.

Figure 8-2   Signal conversion by controller.

responsibility. Because it has processing capability, it is often referred to as a Front End Processor (FEP).

Some of the functions that may be performed by a communications controller are:

- Converting signals from the processor to the modem from parallel by bit, serial by byte (character) to serial by bit and byte, and vice versa (see Figure 8-2)
- Speed conversion: channel and line speeds are different
- Error detection using character and block parity checking
- Identification of control characters
- Buffering and queueing data
- Polling
- Data link control, involving synchronization and identifying the source and destination of a transmission
- Conversion to a standard protocol

The software that may be found in a communications controller are Emulation Program (EP) or Network Control Program (NCP). There is also a possible replacement for EP (NSI—Non-SNA Interconnection), and an NCP option, PEP (Partitioned Emulation Program), which permits an NCP and EP to co-exist.

Modem   A modem must be connected at each end of a telephone line. The function of the modem is to convert the digital signals to audio frequency signals that can be transmitted, and convert the analogue signal from the phone line back to digital. Modem is short for modulator–demodulator, which refers to its two conversion functions.

Modems may modulate a wave in one of three ways:

• Amplitude
• Frequency
• Phase

Modems can also use a combination of amplitude and phase modulation. Amplitude and frequency are illustrated in Figure 8-3; phase modulation is the method of signaling that indicates a 1 or 0 by changing the phase (direction) of the wave by 0°or 180°.

Protocols are the rules used by two connected devices to communicate intelligibly. The three main protocols in use are:

• Start-stop
• Binary Synchronous (BSC)
• Synchronous Data Link Control (SDLC)

SDLC allows faster communication and is more commonly used.

Telecommunications Network   Telephone lines can either be switched or dedicated. A switched line will be established when a number is dialed and answered. The route used by the line will change each time the connection is made, and line quality, therefore, may be variable. A dedicated or leased line is a permanent link between two parts of a network. It typically allows faster transmission rates and may allow duplex communication.

The speed of communication along a line is given in bits per second or baud. These are not strictly the same, as baud means the rate at which changes can be made in the signaling condition of a circuit: they only correspond when two-condition signaling is used.

Cluster Controller   A cluster controller (e.g., IBM 3274) will take the serial transmission from the modem, ensure data integrity, and pass it to the appropriate screen. It will take transmissions from the terminal and organize them for sending on to the modem.

Terminal   The terminal is most frequently a CRT-type device like an IBM 3178 or 3179, which the user will use both for input and output.

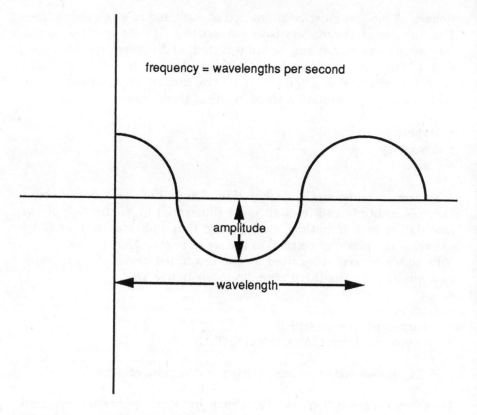

Figure 8-3   Diagram of a sound wave.

Alternatively, the terminal may be a printer like an IBM 3287, which can be used for output only.

Software Components

Being originally designed as a development tool for programmers and as an interactive system for academic and scientific applications made VM unique from IBM's other systems, which were mainly batch oriented. Two of the original four components of VM (CMS and RSCS) were directly concerned with communication. CMS (Conversational Monitor System) is an interactive system which includes an editing facility. RSCS (Remote Spooling Communication Subsystem) is a batch data transfer system. (For completeness, the other two components are CP and IPCS.)

Initially, VM supported teletype terminals and so offered ASCII support (and still does). With the introduction of the 3270 family of terminals, support for local and remote (EBCDIC) terminals was added. Local non-SNA terminals were at first supported, and later remote point-to-point terminals were added.

VM/XA supports only local non-SNA 3270 systems.

Passthrough (PVM) with its 3274 emulation facilities allowed VM, VSE, and MVS machines to be connected in a BSC network. It also introduced multipoint BSC 3270 support and switched point-to-point support.

VM/SP release 2 introduced the DIAL command, which allowed users to DIAL from remote terminals to gain access to Passthrough. Access from Passthrough to the local VM system was achieved via Passthrough's use of VM's logical device support. It allowed CICS (running under a guest operating system) and CMS users to use the same terminal. Returning to CMS from CICS was a problem.

Both RSCS and Passthrough are BSC-based protocols allowing multiple CPUs to participate in a network. The main drawbacks are:

• Non-SDLC protocol, therefore non-SNA
• The control of the basic communications functions takes place in the CPU rather than in the FEP, causing a performance overhead.
• BSC is a point-to-point protocol and has an extra overhead if networked.

IBM's RSCS version 2 product enhanced VM connectivity by allowing VM spool files to be sent to or from:

• Another VM system running RSCS via a CTCA (Channel To Channel Adaptor) or a BSC line
• A VSE system running POWER Networking via a CTCA or BSC line
• An MVS system using JES via a CTCA or a BSC line
• A 2780 or 3780 Remote Job Entry (RJE) terminal via a BSC line
• An RJE station or HOST using HASP or ASP protocols via a BSC line
• Printing of spool files on non-SNA 3270 printers

When used in conjunction with VTAM, RSCS also supports spool file transfer to/from:

- Another RSCS/VTAM system
- An MVS system using JES and VTAM
- A VSE system using POWER Networking and VTAM
- Printing of spool files on SNA 3270 printers

RSCS´ can also be used as an intermediate node for forwarding spool files to a third or subsequent node. RSCS Networking is the latest RSCS version. It is based on IBM's own VNET.

VTAM RSCS Network Application (VRNA) was a set of add-ons to RSCS release 2. It allowed data to be routed to the VRNA application running in VSE or VS1 (i.e., no MVS support).

VTAM (Virtual Telecommunications Access Method) was originally a rewrite of BTAM with many of the interfaces simplified. VTAM is essentially a network management product. Line management is moved from the application (as in BTAM), and a special application to manage all the communication facilities is provided. The access method is a set of subroutines designed to transfer data to and from the management application. It was used originally on MVS and VSE systems.

VTAM with VM has always been less than straightforward. Virtual Communication Network Application (VCNA) was introduced to implement a VM/VTAM interface. It allowed entry into any system (VM, VSE, MVS) from a remote terminal. It has a prerequisite of a VSE or VS1 (not MVS) guest operating system. VCNA would execute under the guest operating system rather than under VM directly. VCNA communicates with the CCS (Console Communications Services) feature of VM/SP using the Inter-User Communication Vehicle (IUCV), and CCS interfaces with the usual VM routines. In this way CMS appears to be communicating with an ordinary terminal.

VM/SP release 4 offered VTAM support without the need for a guest operating system. ACF/VTAM release 3 runs under GCS (Group Control System), which is considered by some to be a cutdown version of MVS. GCS uses the CMS file system and it provides recovery facilities for failing machines. VTAM runs in a VTAM service machine (VSM).

GCS makes use of VCNA, which has been repackaged as VSCS (VM SNA Console Support). VSCS is a VTAM application that runs alongside VTAM in the same virtual machine. VTAM controls I/O and, therefore, bypasses the VM I/O routines. VTAM handles terminals, CTCAs, and FEPs. VTAM will route data to another node, which can be either VTAM in a guest operating system or VSCS. VSCS passes data via IUCV to CCS. CCS then passes the data to

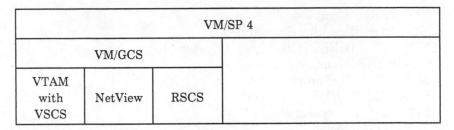

Figure 8-4   Relationship between VTAM and VM.

the appropriate virtual machine to which the user is logged on. The relationship between VTAM and VM is illustrated in Figure 8-4.

VM/SP release 5 introduced TSAF (Transparent Services Access Facility) as a vehicle for LU 6.2 connections or APPC/VM (Advanced Program-to-Program Communication). Each processor has to have a TSAF service machine. Communication can be BSC, via a CTCA or a LAN.

AVS is the VTAM version of TSAF available with release 6. It stands for APPC/VM VTAM Support and allows communication through an SNA link.

VM/XA SP release 2 provides GCS support, although this support is not available with release 1.

The current version of PVM no longer has a 256-line limit and can use multidrop lines.

ISPF (Interactive System Productivity Facility), which is an easy to use menu-driven system for CMS users, runs in a service machine and uses VMCF (Virtual Machine Communication Facility) to communicate between this and ISPF in a user machine.

IUCV is the part of CP that manages communication among programs, either between virtual machines (on the same processor) or between virtual machines and CP.

VMCF is part of CP and allows virtual machines to send and receive data to and from other virtual machines.

NetView is an SNA (Systems Network Architecture) network management tool and is a collection of management software and procedures incorporating the functions of NCCF (Network Communication Control Facility), NPDA (Network Problem Determination Application), NLDM (Network Logical Data Management), and others.

Communication Software   The following lists some of the third-party communication software that is available to run under VM. The main supplier is given in parentheses following the product name.

- CA-VTERM (Computer Associates)
- Multiterm (Blue Line Software)
- NETWORK DIRECTOR (Phoenix Systems)
- PASSPORT (MacKinney Systems)
- SIM/SESSION (Simware)
- SWITCH/VM (BMS Computer)
- TPX (Legent Corporation)
- TUBES (Macro 4)
- VIRTUE (Westinghouse)

MEASURING NETWORK PERFORMANCE

There are a number of sources that can be used to find out how the network is performing. These include network professionals, users, and monitors.

Professionals who control the day-to-day running of the network will have an idea about whether or not it is doing what it is supposed to. They are able to judge from the number of user complaints, other comments, hardware reliability, and experience.

The users will always have some idea of their average response time or of how long it takes to do a print run or other similar task. They will also know how often the system was "down," though of course, if the terminal, the host, or something in-between fails, the problem is all the same to them and on many occasions they will not have realized that it was "back-up" until some time after it actually was.

There are a range of products that monitor the performance of the network as a whole or its individual parts. These can be used to get a picture of the performance of the network. In addition, there are a number of tools available that monitor the performance of individual parts of the network. These are usually hardware monitors.

NETWORK MONITORS

Network monitors fall into three distinct groups. They are:

- Line monitors
- Network control systems
- Performance measurement systems

Line Monitors

An example of a line monitor is a datascope, which although primarily a diagnostic device, can be used on a single line to monitor certain aspects of performance, such as error rates, polling cycles, etc. Sophisticated models can be programmed to identify certain events, count them, or time the intervals between predefined events. Many datascopes can record the sequences for subsequent playback and analysis.

Network Control Systems

Network control systems allow the user to monitor the network for failure. They usually contain alarm facilities, which warn operators when a failure has occurred. They also usually allow diagnostics to be run, which can lead to isolation of the faulty component and rapid corrective action. This helps maintain the availability of the network.

Performance Measurement Systems

Performance measurement systems are designed as both real-time alerting tools and as data collection devices for historical reporting to aid configuration management and capacity planning functions.

NCCF NCCF (Network Communication Control Facility) is associated with VTAM and allows checking to take place of:

• A line
• A control unit
• A device

It can also be used to stop and restart devices. It is now incorporated into NetView.

NLDM NLDM (Network Logical Data Manager) executes under NCCF and is concerned with logical problem diagnosis; i.e., it can be used to diagnose software problems. It tracks each session by recording:

- Session activation
- Data flow
- Session deactivation

Support for RTM (Remote Terminal Monitor) is included in NLDM. NLDM is now incorporated into NetView.

NPDA NPDA (Network Problem Determination Application) places into a database statistics about errors from hardware devices via NCCF. These devices include:

- Communications controllers
- TP links
- Terminals

Using the database, it is possible to obtain an indication of which components are failing. NPDA is now incorporated into NetView.

WHAT TO MEASURE

The measurements required from any network fall into four categories. These are:

- Errors
- Throughput analysis
- Response time
- Cost

Although cost is not a technical measurement, it is affected by the other three interrelated factors. The interrelationship can be summarized as follows. As the number of errors (line errors and failures) increases, throughput and response times worsen and the cost (for a similar workload) increases.

Line throughput and response time are closely related. As line utilization increases, response times increase, but there is a cut-off point at which the resultant service becomes unacceptable to most users. A compromise that provides acceptable throughput and response while also being reliable and within budget is usually required.

Errors

Error measurement is usually divided into two categories—failures and errors. Typically, failures are the most easily identified and most commonly monitored.

Failures may occur on any part of a computer system and network, although to a terminal user a failure in any one of a number of components will have the appearance of the computer being down.

If the host or FEP fails, there will usually be some sort of internal alarm or message to the operator's console to this effect. Typically, the effects are so widespread that the problem is addressed with great speed.

A failure of a modem or line can be isolated by signal monitoring of the V24 interface signals. This means that if the carrier drops, an alarm will be sounded and the network operators can take the appropriate action, such as changing the modem or switching in another line. The techniques range from basic signal monitoring/alarming to patching with alarm, automatic electronic switching, and fault reporting.

The Network Problem Determination Application (NPDA) provides alerts on lines going down, but this is restricted to those users with authorized access. In addition to this, a combination of NPDA, NCCF, and NLDM (or NetView if installed) will provide historical data on what happened just before the failure and provide recommended courses of action for problem rectification.

Hardware performance monitoring systems always provide this type of alerting, generally using color displays to present network status information in real time, although different manufacturers may represent the information in different ways.

Other hardware problems, i.e., control unit and device failure, are usually reported by signal monitoring techniques. IBM software tools do alert regarding control unit and device failure, and hardware performance monitors will usually detect control unit failure due to lack of response to polls from the host; however, due to their central site position, they cannot detect a remote device failure.

The monitoring of line errors as distinct from line failures cannot be done by pure signal monitoring but needs analysis of the traffic on the line in order to detect that messages have been received incorrectly and must therefore be retransmitted.

Some hardware tools will produce data on messages retransmitted, e.g., some datascopes can be programmed to count all retransmitted frames (but only on one line at any one time). More sophisticated systems provide this information across multiple lines along with traffic information such as characters and messages sent and received.

IBM's combination of NPDA, NCCF, NLDM, or NPM (NetView Performance Monitor) give information relating to line errors and will give an alert when threshold values are exceeded. NPM gives information about the messages and bytes retransmitted due to error, plus the number of polls not receiving a response and the number of message timeouts.

Hardware performance monitors can give real-time alerts in full color when threshold values for messages retransmitted are exceeded, and similarly for polls not receiving any response.

Other statistics that can be usefully calculated include the Mean Time To Recover (MTTR) from a failure and the Mean Time Between Failures (MTBF) for a particular component. These results can be used to indicate how reliable any particular component on the network is.

Throughput Analysis

Throughput analysis is the process of monitoring the traffic on the line to assess whether the expected throughput is being attained and also to see how other factors such as line errors and user response times are affected.

A count of the number of messages or frames together with their associated sizes is required. This can be used to produce an overall count of the total number of characters and messages both sent and received. Ideally these counts should include a separate count for the number of polls on the line and should separate the data from the protocol overhead. Another useful measurement at this point is a count of the number of separate devices actually in use and a note of which ones they are. It is worth knowing which terminals are heavily used and which are largely ignored.

Measurement of line loadings, error measurements, and information on front-end processor usage, buffer lengths, etc. can be used to find line utilization over average periods and at peaks. Line utilization can be considered in one of two ways.

$$Line\ utilization = \frac{number\ of\ bits\ sent\ and\ received}{line\ speed} \qquad (1)$$

This means that if 4800 characters are sent down a 9600 line in 1 second, the line utilization is 50 percent.

Although this is a reasonable representation of line utilization, it takes no account of the fact that in a polled environment time is inevitably taken by propagation, modem turnaround, etc., where the line is simply not available. Therefore, line utilizations above 60 percent, in practice, are unlikely over significant periods.

In situations where polling takes place across satellite links in half duplex mode, line utilizations much above 30 percent are unlikely.

$$line\ utilization =$$
$$\frac{no.\ of\ bits\ sent\ and\ received}{line\ speed} + percent\ of\ time\ line\ unavailable \qquad (2)$$

This, however, is very difficult to measure, and capacity planning staff should have an idea of the maximum practical line utilizations based on individual line characteristics.

Response Time

Poor response time comes second to line failure as the most visible symptom of poor network performance. In most cases the user does not care about errors and throughput as long as the response to his terminal is good.

One definition of response time is "the response that the user sees," i.e., from the time when the user depresses the 'enter' key to the full response being displayed on the screen.

Response time is made up of a number of components. These are:

• The delay due to waiting for poll within the controller
• The delay due to the inbound message traveling down the line
• The host delay (some host-based software monitors call this response time), which includes delays due to front-end processors
• The delay due to outbound travel back to the terminal

What is Available to Measure Response Time? Overall response time can be measured from the terminal by using a stopwatch, but there is no way of knowing where the delays are occurring.

If a datascope is sophisticated enough, it may be possible to program it in such a way as to collect all the above timings, but there will be no facilities for storing or alarming on the data.

NPM does produce figures for response time, both internal and external, but the external values, i.e., the link delays, are statistical values rather than definitive measures. NPM time stamps some of the path-ins that require a response from the controller and measures the delay until the response is received.

RTM (Remote Terminal Monitor) can be used, but it entails a hardware upgrade to those 3274 control units that are to be monitored. The 3274 is then able to monitor response time as seen by the user and the summary information is sent to NLDM in the host upon request. Reports may be produced daily from this data.

The performance measurement systems mentioned give real-time alerting upon response time or host delay degradation against users. They will also collect summarized archive data at user-selectable time intervals, down to individual device or application levels.

Using this data a picture of the response time perceived by every user on the network at any time of the day or night can be built.

With this type of system it is possible to:

• Have real-time information for operational management
• Verify users' complaints and rectify them
• Rectify configuration problems such as bottlenecks
• Accurately plan upgrade paths using archive information

MEASUREMENT BY APPLICATION

Once it is possible to measure what is happening on a network (line errors, loadings, response times, etc.) it is useful to know:

• What people are doing on their terminals
• What applications they are accessing
• If long response times are associated with a particular application or if it is general bad response
• If applications are being used to the expected degree

It is important from a performance management standpoint to be able to differentiate between different types of transactions. It may be that a particular transaction type causes an unacceptably long response time and has a noticeable impact on other users on the line.

A further aspect of measurement by application involves the managed addition of new applications. A company cannot afford to risk a new application having a disastrous impact on their network. It is necessary to test the effect of new applications when they are added so that they can be withdrawn if they cause serious deterioration of performance.

HINTS AND TIPS

The real key to improving the performance of the network is to understand exactly what is going on. Four suggestions are given below that should improve a user's terminal performance.

- The SET REMOTE ON command as an XEDIT option could be used to improve response times on remote 3270 terminals.
- Entry Assist can be used to improve productivity when working at 3270 terminals.
- With HPO release 5 there are forward and backward options on the PF key retrieve (SET PF RET BACK/FORW). This can be useful to retrieve the previous command from the buffer.
- With HPO release 5, VTAM terminals can use the TERM BREAKIN GUESTCL command. This prevents XEDIT sessions being interrupted by messages. The terminal will bleep but remain in full-screen mode.

9

Subsystems

The VM control program will act as a hypervisor allowing a number of virtual machines to run on the hardware under it. Although tuning of VM itself is important to get the optimum throughput from it, there may be company needs specifying that a particular virtual machine is to get more than its fair share of resources. For example, if VTAM and GCS are given a high priority, it will minimize delays experienced by remote terminal users. Many performance improvements for individual virtual machines can be achieved using SET commands (see Chapter 6).

This chapter looks at the most frequently installed or most important systems that can be installed under VM. This is to provide performance managers with at least an overview of how the systems work, why they are important, and how they relate to VM itself. The chapter also includes suggestions as to how the performance of these systems could be improved.

The systems are:

- CMS
- Guest operating systems (VSE and MVS)
- CICS
- Relational database (SQL/DS is used as an example)
- PROFS

CMS

The Conversational Monitor System (CMS) is an interactive single-user operating system. On a typical VM system there will be a large number of CMS users. Each CMS user will be allocated his own virtual machine with all the appropriate virtual devices, including minidisks. The user can enter CMS commands, or CP commands that will be passed to the control program. If a command is entered from a terminal or from an EXEC, a search sequence is carried out to find the instruction to be performed. This is shown in Figure 9-1.

CMS is stored as a saved system. Each user must IPL their own version of it. This can be done by keying in I CMS or by giving the address of the saved system, e.g., I 190. Many users have the command invoked automatically for them by placing it in their directory entry. When a user logs on to CMS, a file called the PROFILE EXEC will be executed. This can contain commands that will be invoked to automatically tailor the user's environment to suit his particular requirements.

There is a wide range of software available to run under CMS, including:

- Report generators
- Sort programs
- File copy utilities
- Problem determination packages (IPCS or DVF)
- CICS
- Screen manager (ISPF)
- Compilers (COBOL, PL/I, Pascal)
- Graphics packages (GDDM)
- Complete application environments (SQL, ORACLE, NOMAD)
- Office automation products (PROFS)

CMS uses XEDIT, which is a powerful file editor, to create and modify files. It also uses the SAA approved REXX (REstructured eXtended eXecutor), which is an interpreted command procedure language. There are also two older procedure languages called EXEC and EXEC2. These can be used like a programming language and like Job Control Language (JCL). The ease with which CMS can be used often leads to poorly designed applications which make inefficient use of the resources available.

CMS can be used to develop and debug programs for use with VM or a guest operating system. There is also a batch facility that can be used for running programs in background mode.

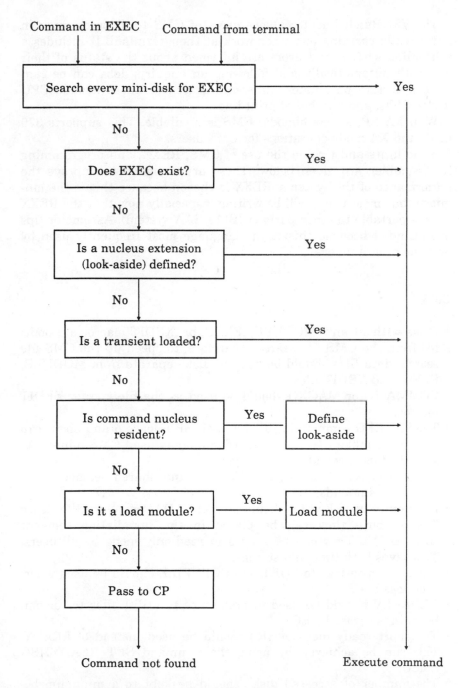

Figure 9-1   CMS command resolution.

The VM Batch Facility allows users of CMS to dispatch work in batch while carrying out other work at their terminal. It includes a scheduling system and users are informed about the status of their jobs both automatically and following an enquiry. Jobs can be canceled if certain parameter values are exceeded. These include CPU usage, SIOs, and number of print lines.

With XA SP, a new bimodal CMS is available. This supports 370 mode and XA mode operations for CMS users.

Some hints and tips on the use of CMS, REXX, and programming in Assembler are given below. These are designed to improve the performance of the systems. REXX is chosen because this is the language that most users will be writing (especially now that the REXX code is portable to other parts of IBM's SAA system). Assembler tips are included because this is the language most frequently used by systems programmers.

CMS

- Disks without any .MODULE, .EXEC, or .XEDIT macros are omitted from the CMS file search. Therefore, to speed up the CMS file search, data files should be kept on disk separate from MODULE, EXEC, and XEDIT files.
- COMMAND or MACRO should be used as the filetype for XEDIT macros.
- The SAVEFD command available with SP release 5 and above can be used to make file directories of commonly used CMS mini-disks shared. This saves I/O and storage.
- The use of NUCXLOAD, EXECLOAD, and shared segments will save program loads.
- Frequently used EXECs should be EXECLOADed. With SP release 5 and above they can be placed in the installation segment (DCSSGEN). They can be shared in read-only mode by all users. This saves both time and storage.
- Faster alternatives to SORT and COPYFILE should be used wherever possible.
- GLOBALV should be used in preference to utility files to remember things across EXECs.
- The short ready message (R;) should be used instead of READY. This can be achieved by using the command SET READYMSG SMSG.
- The number of accessed disks should be kept to a minimum because this reduces the time and effort spent searching for a file.

- Files on the A disk should be stored contiguously and in the order of frequency of use, with the most frequently used ones first.
- With XA SP release 2, CMS mini-disks and the user directory can be cached in expanded storage.

REXX

- Appropriate items should always be enclosed in quotes.
- To avoid lots of unnecessary variables in large programs, DROP should be used.
- Internal subroutine calls are more economic than external ones.
- The ADDRESS command should be used, as this saves the interpreter having to perform synonym resolution or searching for EXECs of the same name before invoking a CMS command.
- EXECUPDT should be used to remove blanks and comments from EXECs, and CMPREXX for REXX. They can then be invoked much faster.

ASM

- CMS I/O should be used because it is faster than I/O simulation.
- A branch to nucleus code is faster than SVCs.
- If external REXX modules are implemented as functions, they should be called RXFUNCTI.

GUEST OPERATING SYSTEMS

Operating systems, most frequently VSE or MVS, can be run as guests under VM. There are a variety of reasons for doing this. Some sites use the guest system in order to host a full function CICS system; others may use VM as an extension to their operating system, to provide the facilities with CMS for program development, or to provide APL facilities. Others may use VM to allow VSE to run on hardware that will not support it in native mode or to provide multiple guest systems on one set of hardware. Some sites may run a guest system to process large batch jobs.

With XA, guest systems can make use of expanded storage for their own paging. Expanded storage can be divided at 1 MB boundaries and attached to any guest system.

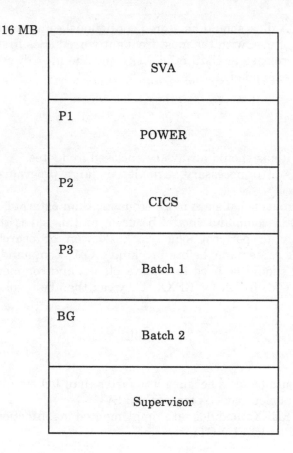

Figure 9-2   Example of VSE version 1 storage layout.

It cannot be stressed too much that at some stage the relative importance of the guest system compared to VM itself must be established. It must also be decided if part of the guest system is more important, for example, a CICS system.

VSE

The Virtual Storage Extended (VSE) operating system was a development from DOS (Disk Operating System) that was available on mainframes. VSE/SP is most suitable for small to medium sized installations. Version 1 can support up to 16 MB of virtual storage, which is subdivided into a number of processing partitions. These

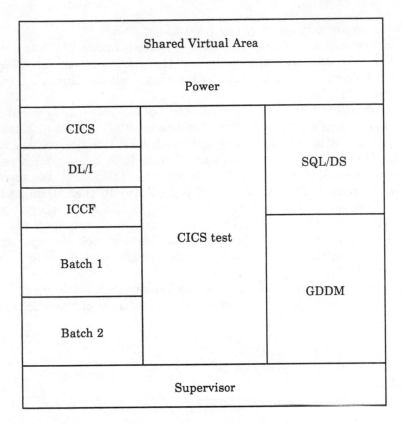

Figure 9-3   Example of VSE version 2 set-up.

can be used to support a batch application or a particular subsystem. This is shown in **Figure 9-2**. The priority of the partitions is the same as the order in which they are placed in the address space, starting from the top. This means that POWER and CICS will get much more service from the system than the BG partition.

Version 2 supports up to three virtual address spaces, each up to 16 MB in size as a way of improving the performance of the system. One of its key features is this Virtual Address Extension (VAE). These extra address spaces could be used for SQL/DS and GDDM or CICS. This is illustrated in **Figure 9-3**.

Version 3 offers support for nine address spaces up to a maximum of 128 MB. This in many ways reduces the need for VSE sites to run multiple copies of VSE under VM. Version 4 offers a number of extended facilities.

There are, in general, very few ways to tune VSE.

VSE systems are usually run as V=V guests under VM, but with the new VAE code available with VSE there is no reason why they could not be run V=R and gain the benefits available through using PMA (see Chapter 5).

With multiple VSE systems, the method of lock-file management is a cause of much criticism. VSE will create multiple I/Os to disk each time a user attempts to access a record. The lock-file resides on shared DASD and controls access to all records. A request for a record will cause VSE to generate an instruction to the lock file to retrieve the record. The record is then locked. Any further attempts to access that record will be rejected by the lock-file and a short wait follows before VSE can try again. Heavy contention usually leads to frequent waits and this can be compounded by the lock-file reporting false lock conditions. This problem is due to the poor hashing technique used.

A number of products are available that can be used to overcome this problem and thereby improve the performance of the VSE systems. The products include:

• Cache Magic LF from SDI
• Extend/VSE from Goal Systems
• Softkey from Jeyco
• Vlock/VM from Blue Line Software

MVS

MVS is used mainly at medium to large installations. It currently comes in three versions. These are:

• MVS/SP version 1, which can address up to 16 MB. (This is illustrated in Figure 13.)
• MVS/SP version 2 or MVS/XA (eXtended Architecture), which can address up to 2 gigabytes. (This is illustrated in Figure 9-4.)
• MVS/SP version 3 or MVS/ESA (Enterprise Systems Architecture), which can also address up to 2 GB, and can additionally make use of dataspaces and hyperspaces.

Each version can make use of an almost unlimited number of address spaces available. (The actual limit is specified in the system parameter library—a file called SYS1.PARMLIB.)

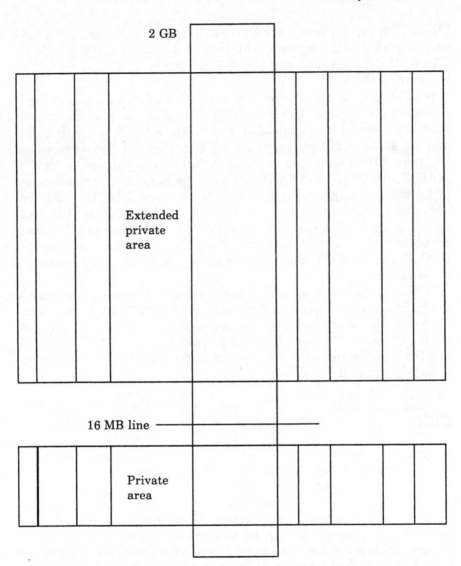

Figure 9-4   Example of MVS/XA address space layout.

The MVS address space is made of three areas: the system or nucleus area, the common area, and the private area. The system area contains the resident nucleus programs necessary to make the MVS system function as MVS. The common area is also shared by all the address spaces. It contains pageable programs that are used frequently by executing tasks (Pageable Link Pack Area) and control blocks. The private areas are allocated to each TSO user, batch job, and started task. Programs that execute in private areas include VTAM, JES2, initiators, and CICS. Batch jobs will execute in initiator address spaces.

With MVS there is far more that can be tuned and there is greater control of the system than with VSE. Operators have a vast repertoire of commands that can alter the characteristics of a particular address space or of the system as a whole. Many of these overwrite (for that session only) the values specified in the parameter library (PARMLIB). Within the PARMLIB partitioned dataset are a number of members that are used to define the system. IEASYS calls the appropriate members to be used. IEAIPS in particular contains values that are used by the Systems Resource Manager (SRM) when scheduling work. Other members that pass values to the SRM are IEAICS and IEAOPT. Performance tuning is achieved by changing these values.

MVS is usually run as a V=R guest in order that its performance not be reduced by very much due to the overhead of VM. Its performance can also be enhanced by the use of PMA. Other techniques include dedicating channels to MVS so that VM is unaware of them and letting MVS use part of expanded storage for its own paging and thereby improve its performance.

CICS

Interactive or online systems like CICS (Customer Information Control System) are designed to allow a large number of users to access a database concurrently from terminals.

The system may be menu-driven, i.e., the user selects an option from a menu which calls a program; or command-driven, i.e., the user calls the program directly by entering a command.

Terminal users enter 4-character transaction identifiers, which are linked to a piece of application program. Programs tend to fall into one of three categories:

• Online inquiry
• Online inquiry with update
• Online data entry

CICS allows multitasking, which means that more than one task (i.e., unit of application program for a specific user) can be executing at a given time.

CICS systems are usually run under VSE or MVS. It is also possible to link a CICS system in one VSE system to another CICS system under a different VSE system. This uses the Inter-System Communication (ISC) facility. With MVS CICS, address spaces can be linked using the Multi-Region Operation (MRO) facility.

CICS is made up of four components:

* Managements, or control, programs
* Tables
* Control Areas
* Application programs

The *managements* control different areas of CICS, e.g., terminal management or file management. The *tables* define the CICS environment, e.g., a list of all the application programs available (PPT) or a list of all the files available (FCT). The *Control Areas* are used by CICS while it is executing to keep track of what's going on. The *application programs* are either user-written or bought as a package and invoked directly by the user. These programs perform the work that needs to be done. The other CICS components are an overhead necessary to allow these programs to execute.

Application programs running in CICS issue CICS commands; an example for a COBOL program might be:

```
EXEC CICS  ....
   function option 1 (argument)
           option 2 (argument)
   END-EXEC
```

Overview of Sequence of Events

Terminal management will move any input from a user's terminal to an area inside the CICS address space or partition. Task management will check that the user has entered a valid transaction identifier by checking it against the entries in the Program Control Table (PCT). The task is assigned a priority up to 255 and waits until it is selected to continue. Program management locates the application program and passes control to it. If the program wants to use datasets, file management checks the file control table to ensure that the files exist, that the files are open, and that the user is authorized to access them. A copy of the file is placed in a file input area inside CICS. The parts of the file required by the user are copied from the file input area to the terminal input/output area, and then terminal management will write it to the user's terminal.

CICS performance can generally be improved by paying careful consideration to the placement and arrangement of files (in particular VSAM key sequenced file data and index components) and sensible scheduling of batch work.

CICS/VM

A recent development for CICS is the introduction of CICS/VM, which allows CICS to run directly under VM (or, more exactly, under CMS) and not use a guest operating system. Associated with CICS/VM are a number of benefits and drawbacks.

On the negative side, the performance of CICS/VM seems to be quite inferior to its MVS or VSE equivalents. It has been estimated that maximum transaction rates would be in the range of 50 to 60 per minute compared to a typical maximum in excess of 200 per minute with the MVS or VSE versions.

A second disadvantage relates to the file access. This is achieved through the use of server machines, either VSAM or SQL/DS. If the CICS system is to make use of Transient Data or Temporary Storage, then SQL/DS becomes a prerequisite because these functions are implemented using SQL/DS, and this may incur a site in extra (unplanned) expenditure. Additionally, it will only allow access to data held at a remote site if that data is managed by a CICS system.

Thirdly, there is no support for older macro level systems which might prevent VSE or MVS CICS users throwing away their guest systems and running all CICS application under CICS/VM.

Many people consider the implementation of CICS/VM as a CMS application, rather than in a virtual machine controlled by GCS, to be a disadvantage. However, this implementation does lead to many of the advantages offered by the system. For example, a user need not be aware of the difference between the CMS and CICS environments. Additionally the user need only log-on once to the CMS user-id and not have to reenter a user-id and password when entering the CICS environment. This will be achieved either from a menu or by entering a CMS command.

An advantage from the point of view of the systems programmers is the way the CICS/VM is maintained. The use of tables has been replaced by panel definitions, and the whole process is thereby simplified.

Also on the positive side is the advantage offered to the program developer. With MVS or VSE versions of CICS it is possible to write to various parts of storage within the CICS partition. Sometimes this will overwrite code that is already stored there, because CICS does not offer any kind of storage protection. Storage violations of this kind are not a problem with CICS/VM because running under CMS, each application runs in its own virtual machine and, therefore, program isolation is automatic.

In general, CICS/VM does not seem to be a complete replacement for the MVS or VSE versions of CICS but might be of use to those 10–20 percent of VM sites that do not run a guest system. The simplifications probably make it an acceptable product for those sites with limited systems programming experience that would be expecting to install VM/IS as their operating system. Even so, there are clearly still difficulties for these sites to overcome.

SQL/DS

Many VM sites have a database installed. A database is defined as a structured collection of related data. A distinction is usually drawn between the "logical" and "physical" view of the data, and the logical view can be further refined along lines suggested by Ted Codd. SQL/DS (Structured Query Language/Data System) is an example of a relational database, and it is installed at more VM sites than any other relational database.

SQL/DS is IBM's relational database and is used on medium-sized systems using VM or VSE. The VM version of SQL/DS is almost identical to the VSE version. It is also very similar in concept to the MVS DB2 system. At VM sites SQL/DS runs under CMS.

SQL/DS supports the relational or normalized data model through the SQL language, which allows tables to be defined and maintained and data within the tables to be queried, created, updated, and deleted. Unfortunately, SQL does not support referential integrity, and this vital job is left to the user. SQL/DS does support most of the other requirements of a database, for example, data independence, recovery, and restart, etc.

SQL/DS really only performs well for "query-only"-type databases, where the data is imported from another sytem and remains stable and nonvolatile, rather than operational-type databases.

Within a VM/CMS environment it is possible, and generally recommended, to run multiple SQL/DS databases. Each database is a separate virtual machine with its own mini-disks that are managed entirely by SQL/DS. Care should be taken that no attempt is made to use them as CMS mini-disks. SQL/DS uses these mini-disks for three purposes:

- The directory—a single mini-disk, which is used as a "bit map" to locate data.
- DBEXTENTS—one or more mini-disks, which are used to store the data within the tables.
- Log mini-disk(s)—SQL/DS logs all changes in case of failure.

Other virtual machines communicate with a database machine via the IUCV. A virtual machine currently can be connected to only one database machine at any one time. This means that it is impossible to support distributed processing, where applications can share data from one or more tables which reside in one or more databases.

Each SQL/DS virtual machine is referred to as a server. SQL/DS has multitasking code and uses VM Block I/O to allow it to support more than one requesting machine. Multiple CMS users through the IUCV mechanism make their requests known to the SQL/DS server machine which, again using IUCV and the *BLOCK-IO CP service, accesses the database. Each server machine can own many database extents, and a CMS user can access multiple DBSPACES in any one server machine. The number of concurrent requesting machines is limited by the number of "real agents," which are defined to SQL/DS, although SQL/DS can handle more than this number in terms of connections. A real agent will require 200K of virtual storage to support it. A real agent is in use only when a logical unit of work (LUW) is running. An LUW will last from the start of the first SQL statement executed and includes all subsequent SQL statements until the user issues a commit work statement. Therefore, it is good practice to ensure that LUWs are kept as short as possible; otherwise the need for real agents will be higher, which in turn will increase demands on virtual storage. For screen-based applications it is generally thought best to never let an LUW run over a terminal I/O. Unfortunately, products like ISQL do not always obey this condition.

In addition to real agents, SQL/DS puts demands on VM paging by using virtual storage buffers to hold frequently referenced data. The size of these buffers can be controlled by the systems programmers. The larger the buffers the less real DASD I/O that will be required. However, if they are too large, this will increase the VM paging rate and cause both VM and SQL/DS performance degradation. If SQL/DS is paged by VM, the whole database and all connected users will stop processing.

Some hints and tips on the installation and use of SQL are given below:

- Multiple SQL/DS databases should be installed in separate virtual machines, each with its own databases, and other machines should be allowed to communicate with it using IUCV.
- A DCSS should be used with multiple SQL/DS server machines.
- Two or three single thread server machines should be implemented if one is likely to become a bottleneck. This is easier than trying to split usage later.
- SQL should be used for query-only activities as this is what it does best.
- LUWs should be kept small to reduce the amount of virtual storage required.
- SQL-managed mini-disks should not be used as CMS mini-disks.
- Pool usage should be monitored to ensure that it does not fill up, causing a database abend.
- Data access paths are chosen by the optimizer, not the user, and may affect performance. Statistics used by the optimizer are gathered by running a batch job. Running the job may lock out users, causing even worse performance.
- Statistics should be kept up to date.
- The clustered index option should be used.
- The number of indexes used should be kept to a minimum.
- Volatile data should be unloaded and reloaded frequently.
- The use of storage buffers should be maximized.
- The following modules should be made nucleus-resident:
     DMKIUA
     DMKIUE
     DMKIUL
     DMKBIO
- The SET QDROP dbname OFF USERS command should be used to enhance performance.
- Once SQL is up and running, the SET RESERVE command should be used.
- Automatic locking occurs much more often than expected.
- Users need to find out how to get around SQL/DS's many limitations.

PROFS

PROFS (PRofessional OFfice System) is IBM's office automation product for the VM environment and is aimed at a broad spectrum of users, from technical people to managerial users. It is a derivative of IBM's own internal product called NOSS. PROFS is generally well regarded by users, and there are estimated to be worldwide around 3500 PROFS systems supporting approximately 700,000 users. The European PROFS User Group found that the average site has 850 PROFS users. Running VM/XA SP on a 3090-600E, IBM has bench-marked 6000 PROFS users. PROFS runs under CMS.

PROFS offers a user working from a 3270 terminal the following facilities:

- A word processing facility called DW/370, or sometimes the Document Composition Facility (DCF).
- Time management facilities, covering diary facilities calendars and reminder notes.
- Electronic mail facilities, allowing document distribution via RSCS Networking to mailboxes on different PROFS systems.
- Search and retrieval facilities allow documents to be located using search terms entered when the document was created or modified.

PROFS is loaded as a DCSS and runs under CMS. It makes use of XEDIT and ISPF. Each user is provided with a mailbox and can send messages (short notes to another logged on PROFS user), notes (informal communications that are stored in the recipient's mailbox), and documents (which are formal, stored in a central filing system, and logged). PROFS is used primarily for its electronic mail facilities.

The current version of PROFS is version 2.2. In addition to this a user will require PASF which is the PROFS Application Support Feature. This is a set of extensions to PROFS providing task-oriented menus for access to PROFS, to Application System (AS—an integrated decision support tool), and to Query Management Facility (QMF—used to access SQL/DS). It also provides PC to host communication.

Both PROFS and PASF, with the additional software they require to function fully, are available as a packaged solution called SolutionPac Office Series, VM Edition. This is intended as an easy-to-install, quick-to-get-running solution to the problem many sites face when installing new products. PROFS, PASF, and AS are the starting points for users who wish to migrate to OfficeVision (OV/VM). IBM's new integrated office product.

There are a number of problems that users have experienced with PROFS. These include:

- Difficulties with the document database. It is difficult to delete old or unwanted documents. Also, documents are harder to use than notes, although they do provide a permanent audit trail.
- Many users have found DCF hard to use, considering it to be more akin to a programming language. DW/370 goes some way toward helping to overcome this problem.
- The lack of external communications can be a problem for users who would like to send faxes or telexes or even link into other electronic mail systems (e.g., Telecom Gold). This problem can be overcome by using third-party software.
- A lack of advanced features.

The biggest impact on system performance as a whole is caused by users sending notes. These are kept on the spool and cannot be backed up to tape. They fill the spool area, reducing the space that is available for ordinary spool files, and may all be lost in the event of a VM cold start.

With releases of VM below 5, part of the Free Storage Area (FSA) is taken up by each spool file control block, and typical PROFS users generate lots of spool files.

PROFS users who log-on use to 6K of the Free Storage Area. If they do no work while logged on, they are taking away valuable free storage space.

Some hints and tips on the use of PROFS are given below:

- PROFS shared code should be put on a separate actuator from VMSRES.
- PROFS mini-disks should be given dedicated actuators.
- Two or three single-thread server machines should be implemented from the start rather than trying to split usage when one gets overloaded.
- PROFS REORGS should be performed daily.
- Users should be educated to read and remove notes regularly and not to stay logged on when inactive.

10

Monitors

Performance monitoring is an important part of performance management and is the process by which data concerning what is happening on the system can be obtained.

One of the major problems about using a performance monitor is that it cannot give a true picture of how the system was performing before it was activated because the actual usage of the monitor itself will consume some of the CPU resource available.

Software performance monitor packages are designed to make the collected data available to the user in an easy-to-understand format. Using information from the monitors can help to prevent unrealistic expectations about performance being held.

A performance monitor is a tool, and a mistake that is sometimes made is to confuse tools with solutions. It should be realized what tools can do and what the limitations are. For example:

- Tools only process the data.
- Reporting systems do nothing but present.
- Models are only as good as the input.

REASONS FOR USING A MONITOR

Before any tuning of a system can take place, it is necessary to find out exactly what is going on within the system. This process involves

169

the collection of data. Another piece of software may be necessary to interpret and/or analyze and/or report on the collected data. In addition, software can be installed to take account of this information and use it to model the system for future capacity requirements.

A full list of the uses for a monitor are given below:

• Performance and tuning
• Problem analysis
• Exception reporting
• Resource control
• Service levels
• Capacity planning
• Job accounting
• Program usage

The packages available from various suppliers will be able to perform some or all of these functions.

Performance and Tuning

Performance measurement data is required before any change can be made to the system. Once a clear idea has been formed of how the system, or a component part of it, is performing, it is possible to make modifications to the system. Subsequent performance reports will indicate whether there has been any alteration in the system's performance because of the change that had been made. It will indicate if the change was positive or negative. It will also indicate whether there have been any unplanned changes in performance of another system component. For example, improvements to an SQL machine may have an impact on a guest operating system's performance. If that guest is running a CICS system, there could be a lot of CICS users who will be less productive because their terminal's response times are now worse.

When tuning a system it is important to only make one change at a time; otherwise it is impossible to know which change has caused the measurable difference.

Many sites consider the 80/20 rule to hold good. This rule states that 80 percent of the system tuning will be done in 20 percent of the time. The other 20 percent improvement will only come about by devoting 80 percent of the time to it. With this in mind they usually stop attempting any improvements once the system is running at an acceptable level.

The other problem with fine tuning is that the workload and configuration of the system are likely to change with the passage of time, and any work done today is likely to be invalidated within a short period of time.

Problem Analysis

Problem analysis will typically involve the use of the real-time facilities of a monitor to permit the identification of bottlenecks or other problems on the system as soon as they occur.

Bottlenecks are principally associated with CPU, main storage, paging, and I/O.

Some packages will allow the users of the monitor to write routines to respond to particular problems. Other packages will give tentative explanations of the cause of the problem. Typically, these type of packages will use graphics to make analysis easier.

Some packages have the facility to allow historical data to be replayed through the real-time system. This means that if the exception reporting part of the package has identified a problem from the previous session, the data can be analyzed interactively.

Exception Reporting

There are basically two types of exception reports. These are historic and on-line. When a problem occurs on the system or a preset threshold is exceeded, a warning message can be sent to a log file, or it can be sent to a particular user. In the first instance it would be historic reporting because the message would not be seen until much later by someone reviewing what had happened in terms of performance for that day. In the second case it would be an on-line report and the user receiving the message could take action to relieve the problem.

Resource Control

It is possible to control the utilization of resources if the current use of them is measured. If users are taking more than their fair share of resources, it is possible to send them warning messages, or degrade their performance, or FORCE them off.

Some resource control packages will allow the control of users based on time of day. It is also possible to restrict the usage of a particular virtual machine to a fixed amount of CPU per month. It is always a good idea to inform the Help Desk (or Information Centers where they exist) that a restriction is being applied.

Service Levels

At sites where the DP department is considered to be offering a service to user departments (a process usually associated with internal financial transactions), it is common to find that there are formal service-level agreements between the DP department and the other departments. These service level agreements will contain agreed levels of service that the DP department must provide to these other departments. The use of a monitor will produce information that can be used when drawing up these service-level agreements. In this way the agreements can be realistic in the levels that they promise to provide. The use of a monitor will also show just how well these service levels have been adhered to.

Capacity Planning

The analysis of current machine's workloads and usage can be used to predict future requirements. Simplistic predictions assuming linear growth have typically been replaced by more sophisticated packages. This is the primary function of the capacity planner and will avoid the need for the type of crisis management that can occur as the system lurches from one problem to another.

Another function of the capacity planner is to suggest ways that work can be rescheduled to avoid bottlenecks or contention. It may be possible to restrict development and testing to certain periods of the day, etc.

The data used by capacity planners will take up storage space because it will need to be kept for long periods of time. This is because the data may be analyzed in a number of different ways and may be combined with other data to produce accumulation reports.

Job Accounting

By monitoring what work has been carried out by a user (or job or transaction) it is possible to charge them for each activity. Sometimes there is a requirement for project accounting to take place.

There is a standard (though not very good) facility for job acounting within VM (DMKACNT).

Program Usage

By measuring which programs are used by which people and how often, it is possible to build up a useful picture of system usage. This information can be useful for:

• Determining mini-disk layout
• Deciding if duplicate mini-disks are needed (or caching)
• Grouping users into workgroups
• Deciding how much to charge for the use of certain programs

The problem with this idea is that it is difficult to do. It is possible to modify CMS to report to another virtual machine on each command used. Alternatively, it is possible to select a few commands to be monitored and use EXECs to send the information to a service machine.

TYPES OF MONITOR

Software monitors can be broadly categorized into two groups. These are:

• Online monitors, which basically measure specified resources and report immediately.
• Historical monitors, which collect statistics for later analysis.

Online Monitors

Online monitors are typically run under the control of the operations group. This is because they continually measure system resources and can be used directly for problem determination and system tuning.

Typically, each site will define what criteria they consider to be the basis for acceptable performance. The monitor will compare the values sampled against these predetermined threshold values and report immediately on any deviations. The report will usually be displayed on a screen. Corrective action can be taken immediately to return the system to the preferred state. The main drawback with many online monitors is that they do not have any data storage facilities and, therefore, cannot be used for trend reporting, historical analysis, or capacity planning.

Historical Monitors

Historical monitors sample the state of the system at regular intervals and record the data for later analysis. The most important factors when considering historical monitors is what resources are measured and how often, how the information is presented, and how much control the user has over it.

Monitors may alternatively be classified as either event-driven or time-driven, although there are a few that are a combination of both. Event-driven systems produce records containing status information after any critical events have occurred to a task. Time-driven monitors collect status information at regular time intervals.

CP MONITOR

VM has an internal monitor that can be used to obtain online information about how the system is performing. The information can be obtained primarily through the use of the INDicate and Query commands.

INDicate

The most frequently used INDicate commands are:

- IND FAVOR
- IND I/O
- IND LOAD

- IND PAGing
- IND Queues
- IND USER

IND FAVOR This gives details of users who have had the SET FAVOR command issued for their virtual machine.

IND I/O This shows which users are in an I/O wait and the device for which they are waiting. It can be used to identify where bottlenecks are occurring.

IND LOAD This is a very useful command and provides the following information:

- CPU utilization
- Average number of Q1 and Q2 users
- The ratio of number of pages in store for in-queue virtual machines against the number of available page frames
- A measure of the delay caused by processor and storage contention
- Paging rate
- Percentage of page reads that were associated with a page steal from an in-queue user
- A measurement of system load—a measurement of system time used for page services

IND PAGing This will display users who are in page wait and whether they are on high- or low-speed paging devices. It also includes spooling information, which it does not distinguish from paging information.

IND Queues This allows a user's position within the various system queues to be established. Some of the possible states are given below:

EX—the user is in an instruction simulation wait.

IO—the user is in an I/O wait.

PA—the user is currently executing on the non-IPL processor in an MP environment.

PG—the user is in page wait.

PS—the user is in a PSW wait.

RA—the user is currently executing on an attached processor.

RU—the user is currently executing on the main processor.

All responses to this command are given in priority order within queues, starting with eligible queue one then two, followed by Q1 then Q2.

IND USER This command will provide individual users with information about their execution profile. This will include:

• Page reads/writes
• Page locations
• Resident page count
• Working set size

Query

The most useful of the Query commands are:

• Q SRM SWAPQTIME
• Q SRM PGMACT
• Q SRM MAXPP
• Q SRM DSPSLICE
• Q SRM APAGES
• Q SRM MAXSS
• Q USERS
• Q FRAMES
• Q PAGing
• Q PRIORITY user-id
• Q QDROP

Q SRM SWAPQTIME With HPO up to release 5, Q SRM SWAPQ-TIME will show the actual times that users spend on the interactive and noninteractive swap queues. It can be used as a guide to monitor the way that paging and swapping are being carried out and whether the values specified by the SET SRM SWPQTIME command are being met.

Q SRM PGMACT With HPO, Q SRM PGMACT will show the amount of page migration activity.

Q SRM MAXPP With HPO, Q SRM MAXPP will show the percentage of the preferred paging area that may become full before automatic page migration takes place.

Q SRM DSPSLICE Q SRM DSPSLICE will show the timeslice value that is being used when the dispatcher allocates timeslices to each of the three queues.

Q SRM APAGES Q SRM APAGES will show the number of page frames in the DPA that are available for user pages.

Q SRM MAXWSS Q SRM MAXWSS will show the value for the maximum working set size that is allowed, if any value has been specified.

Q USERS Q USERS command will indicate which virtual machines are logged on at any given time and thereby give a rough indication of how busy the system is.

Q FRAMES With XA, the Q FRAMES command will display how many free storage page frames have been obtained from the Dynamic Paging Area.

Q PAGing Q PAG will display the control variables for paging calculations.

Q PRIORITY user-id Q PRIORITY user-id will display the priority of a particular virtual machine. The lower the value specified, the better the priority of the user.

Q QDROP Q QDROP will display queue drop information.

MONITORS AVAILABLE

The following is a list of the most frequently encountered VM software performance monitors available and their suppliers. (Supplier addresses are given in Appendix 1.)

ADABAS Performance Analysis System from Database Utility Group. This is mainly associated with the DBMS ADABAS, but will allow usage reports to be generated.

BEST/1-VM from BGS is a computer modeling product. It will enable the user to predict future capacity requirements quickly and accurately. It is typically used in association with CAPTURE/VM and CRYSTAL.

CAPTURE/VM from BGS is a system performance reporting and modeling product. It is usually associated with BEST/1-VM and CRYSTAL.

CMAP from VM/CMS Unlimited will measure what is done by CMS machines. This includes performance and user behavior analysis. It can be used stand-alone, but usually the results are input to the SAS system.

CPWATCH from various programmers is a simple but unsophisticated online performance monitor.

CRYSTAL from BGS is an application modeling product for new applications that have not as yet been implemented. It can be linked with BEST/1-VM and CAPTURE/VM.

EXPLORE/VM from Goal Systems contains comprehensive real-time and batch reporting facilities with exception handling. It can be used stand-alone or to produce input for the SAS system.

MICS/VM from Legent Corporation.

OMEGAMON/VM from Candle Corporation checks for potential problems every few seconds and offers in-depth analysis of VM resources. It may be fully customized by means of user-defined screens and menus.

SMART (VM/RTM) from IBM is an online monitor that produces regular reports on key values. It can provide information about thresholds being exceeded.

SIM/SCOPE from Simware.

Vital Signs from Blue Line (Systems Resources in the UK) will allow both online and historical reporting, as well as DASD modeling and exception monitoring. It can be used as input to the SAS system.

VMMAP from IBM is a historical reporting tool that can be used for capacity planning. Although it will store historical data, it cannot archive and reprocess data.

VM MONITOR from Systems Center (VM Software) is an "expert" system designed to evaluate current performance in real time, report on essential system variables, and decide what action is required to improve the system performance. It can also take any necessary action to relieve bottlenecks that it identifies. It is used with VM SORT and VM ARCHIVE.

VM Online Performance Monitor from Adesse will analyze performance problems for individual virtual machines. The information can be tailored for specific analysis situations.

VMPRF (VM Performance Reporting Facility) from IBM can be used with XA SP systems to produce reports on resource and channel usage, response times, throughput, and disk and tape activity.

VPAC from Macro 4 consists of a monitor and data collection component; a resource control component; an online interface for real-time analysis; and data handling and reporting programs. It can be used to take corrective action in the case of a threshold being exceeded. It can be used stand-alone or associated with their System Accounting product.

Watch/VM from BMS.

XAMAP from Velocity Software acts in many ways like VMMAP, but is designed specifically to run on XA systems.

Many of the products can and do make use of the SAS System from the SAS Institute to display the output from the monitor package.

Some sites create their own simple monitoring systems by using the IND LOAD command. This command is placed in an EXEC that loops continually and repeatedly issues the command. The SLEEP command is usually included to ensure that a sensible time occurs between the commands being issued.

SELECTING A PACKAGE

Before selecting a performance monitor the potential purchaser must decide what information he requires from it. He must also decide which of the facilities that are available with each product is a necessary prerequisite for choosing any product, or could be useful in certain circumstances but are not very important, or would not be used in any foreseeable circumstance. Once armed with a "shopping list" of requirements it would be necessary to see how easy the facilities and features of the product were to use by an experienced user and how easy it would be to learn to use the product. Once a short list of possible products had been selected, it would then be necessary to look at the cost of the product. Once all this had been done, an appropriate package would be selected. Full details of the type of questions to ask, in order to evaluate the monitor package, are given later in the chapter.

When testing a product, it is useful if the monitor data itself can be checked for accuracy. This can usually only be done by checking it against another monitor's output.

Cost

Before installing a monitor it is worth considering the costs involved (against cost of not doing it). There are the obvious costs of the software package itself. In addition there is the cost of DASD space necessary to hold both the program and the data it will accumulate. Added on to this is the cost of the CPU cycles, etc., used every time that the program is executed. This may be quite considerable in some circumstances.

The costs given above are usually the ones that appear on the balance sheets. However, there are additional costs to be considered. These additional costs are all to do with staff costs. Before the installation of the monitor it is assumed that all members of staff are fully occupied. If extra work is caused by the monitor's use, i.e., preparing reports or being on hand the whole time to watch the screen, this might result in the need to employ an extra member of staff. A member of staff cannot be doing their old job while using the new monitoring tool. There will be staff costs involved while they are learning to use the system. For example, it may be necessary to pay overtime or employ temporary staff while members of staff are off on training courses to learn how to use the monitor. There might also be payment of expenses for food and lodging while attending these courses.

Balanced against these costs to the company is the unknown figure representing how much better the system's performance will be after the monitor has been in use for a while. This value cannot be quantified until after the product has been in use for at least a year.

Benefits of an Integrated Approach

A haphazard solution using various tools may often prove to be more costly in the long run than an integrated approach. Some products may be incompatible and the results will be inaccurate. The performance analyst will have to learn multiple packages, all of which will have different approaches and methods and philosophies. The advantage of an integrated system is that all the components will share a common methodology and "look" similar. Furthermore, they will not clash with each other and should operate smoothly. Another consideration is that a single source exists for problem reporting and solving at the software product level. This integrated approach is sometimes referred to as "one-stop shopping."

Questions

This section suggests questions that should be asked when selecting a monitor package that will suit the particular requirements of a site. The first set of questions deal with the product itself, the second set deal with the company supplying the product.

Product-related Questions about the product that should be asked are:

• Which versions of VM will it work with?

It is necessary to ensure that not only will the product work with the current version and release of VM that is installed at a site, but that it will also work with any new versions that are likely to be installed, e.g., an SP-to-HPO migration.

• Does the supplier undertake to support the latest announced release of VM?

Although new releases of VM generally add facilities which would, typically, be transparent to the product, support for new VM system features may take time to implement. A user should not be obliged to postpone the installation of new releases for more than three months.

• Are there any software prerequisites?

Some products, for example, require GDDM to function. This would be an additional expense if GDDM were not already installed. When evaluating the product, it is necessary to take into consideration "extras" like this.

• In what form is the package supplied?

If the product is supplied in source form, it must be a language supported at the user's site.

• What steps are involved in modifying the package (either for maintenance or for user modification)?

Almost all packages will, at some time, require some modification. It can be very useful to know how this is done so that an assessment of the workload involved in making changes can be made.

• Are there any user exits or "own code hooks"?

These are the standard means to allow a user to modify a product. Although there are usually restrictions to their usage, they do provide extra flexibility in the use of a product.

• What is involved and how much time does it take to:
  – install the system?
  – tailor the system to individual needs?
  – learn to use the system oneself?
  – train other users?

This will help when deciding how to roster staff to cover for other staff who are involved in any of the above activities.

• Are help facilities incorporated into the product to assist problem determination?

If the product identifies a bottleneck, for example, the inclusion of help facilities will allow the user to choose the appropriate course of action.

• Which hardware resources are monitored/measured?

It is important to know exactly which resources are being monitored. This will ensure that the required ones are being monitored by the package.

• Which software resources are monitored/measured?

As with the previous question, it is important to know exactly what is measured in order to build up a true picture of what is happening in the system.

• Which user workload resources are monitored/measured?

User workload measurements such as throughput and response times at application levels can have an important role in both tuning and capacity planning.

• Is the product event- or sample-driven or both?

Although event-driven monitors are more accurate, they do impose more overhead on the system. Many monitors are a mixture of the two methods.

• Does the system provide any facilities for changing system parameters dynamically?

Some monitors will not only identify problems, but have a range of commands available that allow corrective action to be taken.

• Are there facilities for reporting exceptions based on thresholds set by the user?

To avoid being overwhelmed by data from the monitor, it is useful if reports can be restricted to identifying when user-specified limits are exceeded.

• Is action taken by the product automatically when thresholds are exceeded?

It is possible with some monitors to automatically execute a response to a predetermined situation.

• How are the results presented?

The main options are screen display or hard copy.

• Are reports fixed format or can they be tailored?

If reports can be tailored, this gives more scope to ensure that important information is obvious to anyone reading the report.

• Are graphics supported?

It is easier to derive information quickly from a visual image than words on a page. Therefore, it is useful if graphics are supported. Some monitors have this built in, others use GDDM, while others require an additional package.

- Are graphics in color?

If they are, comparison of data can be done much more quickly.

- Is it possible to model and simulate based on existing data?

In order to predict the future for an installation this can be a useful technique. If discrete simulation is used, this is probably more accurate but heavier on resources than analytical modeling.

- Does the monitor also address the needs of accounting?

While measuring what is going on, the package could be producing data that could be used directly or indirectly as input to a charging algorithm.

- Is the monitor usually run continuously, or is it started and stopped as required?

Different monitors have slightly different requirements. It is worth finding out which type the prospective monitor is.

- What is the overhead of running the system?

At some sites it has been known for the monitor to be turned off during busy periods (when it is most required) because it is consuming too much resource. The supplier should provide figures of resource consumption. These should not exceed 5 percent.

- How much secondary storage is required to hold six months' information?

This will give an indication of the amount of disk storage that will have to be set aside in order to hold the data. This may require the purchase of additional DASD.

Company-related   The following questions relate to the company supplying the software.

- When did the company start?

Investing money with a new company may be risky. If the company is very new, it may be useful to make further inquiries about its financial credentials, in particular, its ability to fund growth without experiencing cash flow problems. A supplier suffering a cash flow crisis is often unable to offer customers the optimum level of support.

• When was the first product installed?

The older a product is, the more likely it is to be stable and (relatively) bug-free. However, the basic design and facilities of newer products may well have benefited from the experience of the pioneers, and they are likely to be at the beginning of their life cycle with more features and facilities to come.

• How many sites have installed the product?

Typically, the number of users is a very good guide to how good a product is. Looked at in conjunction with the first release date and the answers to the next question, the answer to this question should indicate the popularity or otherwise of the product. Also, a product with a large user base is likely to be developed and enhanced more consistently because the funding will be available to cover the development cost; equally, a large user base is a guarantee that the product will continue to be maintained even if the original supplier ceases to support it (for whatever reason)—a large user base will attract some third party to take on the responsibility, whereas a small base will not be so attractive.

• How many new sites have installed the product in the last two years?

Bearing in mind the answer to the previous question, a popular product three or four years ago may not be the best choice today. The success of a product in today's marketplace should be appreciated.

• What is the current version and when was its release date?

If the current release is old, it may be worth waiting for the next release and any new facilities. This could save a later upgrade. However, an old release is probably more stable. If the latest release is recent, it is worth checking how much development has taken place since the previous release; the new release might just be for maintenance purposes. It is also worth finding out the frequency of new releases. If it is more than two a year, it should be examined closely. The supplier's policy in upgrading is also very important. Many suppliers stipulate that at a set time after a release they will not support the earlier release. Caution is advised if a company frequently sends out new releases and has that clause. The supplier's stock answer to many problems is: "Go to the latest release and see if it still occurs."

• Can the product be used stand-alone?

When purchasing a product it is important to establish exactly what facilities are required and whether the product will only function successfully provided that other products (probably from the same vendor) are also purchased.

• What have been the most significant recent developments?

This will establish the current commitment of the supplier to the product.

• What are the company's future plans?

Again, this indicates whether or not the supplier intends to support the product in the future.

• What other areas are addressed by the product?

Some products address more than one area. Knowledge of additional areas covered may well be important in the final selection.

Having established whether or not a package is suitable in terms of operating requirements and functional capabilities, it is worth looking at the supplier's terms—what is provided in the cost, what support is provided, how enhancements and updates are announced, what guarantees are provided, etc.

A computer installation must be able to support and fix problems. Many installations place great emphasis on maintaining strict documentation and standards. The same approach should be adopted when dealing with the product supplier—when a problem is experienced, support must be available to correct it quickly and effectively.

• What support is available?

The supplier's answer should indicate how well they are set up to deal with problems. A product should be avoided if its nearest source of support is geographically remote from its potential purchaser's site. Some vendors have an agreement with a third party. In this case, support should be negotiated separately.

• What training is required, who provides it, where, and at what cost?

The length of training is often an indication of the complexity of the product. Usually, on introduction to a company, training is minimal and free. It is necessary to find out how much it will cost to train people at a later date. If training is available only at a remote location, this adds significantly to the cost of the product. Where courses are provided, this may be as part of the license fee or at additional cost to the customer. In cases where English is not the mother tongue of the installation, it is obviously a definite advantage if courses can be given in other languages.

• What manuals are available?

All suppliers provide manuals, usually in English, to enable the product to be installed and run. The availability of manuals in the language used by the staff at an installation is not only a great convenience, it also indicates that the supplier takes that market sector seriously. However, user documentation written in that language will inevitably be out of date. Finally, it should be stressed that the quality of the documentation is far more significant than the quantity. It is worth getting and browsing through the manuals at an early stage of evaluation.

• Are user references available?

User references should be followed up preferably by telephone or by personal visits rather than by letter. The supplier will naturally tend to select "tame" reference sites, which are sometimes atypical in the use they make of the product and may also receive an unusual amount of support from the supplier. Nevertheless, a lot of useful information can be gained by asking the right questions.

• Does a user group exist?

A user group (even one sponsored by the supplier) can be a useful source of information and advice. It is an effective way for vendors to keep their user base up to date on product developments and to solicit views on how the product should be enhanced.

• Is there a bulletin of product developments?

A regular information bulletin helps to keep a user informed of a product's development, available training courses, forthcoming user groups, meetings, etc.

• Are back levels supported?

The standard policy is to support the last release but one for three or six months after announcement of the current release (i.e., release 1 will be obsolete six months after announcement of release 3). A user with an old release will not be able to use new facilities. However, if a release is stable and the new release only provides support for unrequired features, there should be no compulsion to upgrade immediately.

• Is support available if the package is modified?

Few vendors allow modifications, usually by not allowing access to the source. Where user modifications are possible, the vendors' attitudes will vary enormously. Some suppliers offer support whatever the circumstances, and others will insist that any problem experienced must be repeatable without the modifications. If changes are envisaged, the position regarding support should be carefully checked.

• What are the problem escalation procedures?

This will vary depending upon the size of the vendor's operation, but most suppliers have a procedure for moving or escalating problems through various levels of support to ensure an answer is forthcoming quickly. They should be able to describe these procedures and the timings involved in the escalation. It is worth checking with other users to see how well the vendors perform in this area.

• What warranty is provided?

There should always be some form of warranty from the supplier, e.g., that the package in operation will comply with the reference manual, that compatibility with IBM software will be maintained, etc. Most suppliers now provide a clause in the contract to this effect. If they do not, it should be checked with them, and a clause inserted if they are willing.

• What is the cost of the product?

Obviously a potential user will have to know what the basic costs are before a final decision is made and whether the package can be purchased, leased, or rented. It will depend upon an installation's policy as to the benefits of purchase versus rental. Provided that a maintenance agreement is in force, there should be no difference between purchasing and renting the product. Many products also have chargeable features and these must also be quantified—even though they may not be required. Note that prices vary from country to country, and it is worth checking with local suppliers before a commitment is made to any product.

• What discounts are available?

For multisite installation, e.g., multinational organizations, there are often substantial savings available if all sites install at the same time.

• What implementation support is provided?

One would expect assistance with the installation and an on-site training session with a follow-up after a few weeks.

• What are the maintenance costs?

The annual maintenance charges are typically around 10–15 percent of the current purchase price with the year after purchase-free. If the product is rented or leased, no maintenance should be payable because it is incorporated in the monthly charges.

• Are demonstrations available?

Demonstrations should always be available, but facilities will depend very much upon the size of the vendor and the cost of the product.

• Are free trials available?

Free trials do give an opportunity for the product to be evaluated. If it is easy to install, then it is always worth taking a trial to evaluate whether the product meets all the requirements set for it. Another method adopted by suppliers is to include a "get-out" clause or to charge only a nominal month's rent.

• What are the additional costs?

Apart from the initial installation and new releases, one would usually expect some charge for additional services—training, manuals, modification, etc., and some suppliers do charge an installation fee for their time regardless of whether you use it or not. Users should at least be aware of any potential costs that could be incurred.

• Are there any guarantees in case of supplier ceasing to trade?

This is a safeguard question. If source is not provided, some guarantee must be obtained so that customers do not suffer through problems on the side of the supplier and they will be supplied with all requisite materials if the supplier ceases to trade. Most suppliers will laugh this off, saying that it will never occur, in which case they should have no objections to incorporating a safeguard into the contract.

11

Performance Reports

Associated with performance management are two types of reports. There are the reports produced by the software on the system, and there are the written reports that are to be circulated among the people associated with the system's performance.

Software-produced reports come in two types. The first type are those from online monitors that report what is happening on the system from moment to moment. The second type are those that display information about what has been happening, i.e., from historical monitors.

One important criterion to use when selecting a performance monitor is what information it is important for the monitor to obtain. This involves deciding what the critical system variables are and how often the information should be obtained.

Once the data is being produced by the monitor, it is necessary to use it in some way that will benefit the company. The usual way is to produce reports. This leads immediately to certain questions that need to be answered. These questions are:

- Who is to get a copy of the report?
- What level of information do they need?
- How is the information to be presented?
- How often is the report to be produced?
- What will the report be used for?

TYPICAL INFORMATION

At most sites the same core of data is collected for input into a performance report. This data usually covers such areas as:

- I/O
- CPU usage
- Paging and swapping
- Spooling
- Network
- Data analysis

The following list is only intended to give a brief summary and is by no means presented as complete or exhaustive.

I/O

The type of data about I/O could include such topics as:

- I/O interrupts
- Number of I/Os
- I/O wait time
- I/Os per channel
- I/Os per device

CPU Usage

The type of data about CPU usage could include such topics as:

- TVRATIO for guest systems—total time/virtual time
- Percent CPU utilization
- Time spent in supervisor or problem program state
- Wait states
- Storage utilization

Paging and Swapping

The type of data about paging and swapping could include such topics as:

- Page rates
- Steal rates
- System queue utilization (i.e., Q1, Q2, and Q3)

Spooling

The type of data about spooling could include such topics as:

- Number of print, punch, and reader files
- How full the spool area becomes over time

Network

Typical network measurements will be as follows:

- Response time or host delay
  - average
  - maximum
  - standard deviation
  - number over threshold 1
  - number over threshold 2
- Network delay
- Poll delay
- Number of transactions

Data Analysis

It would also be useful if the data collected on a systemwide basis could be analyzed by:

- Time
- Virtual machine
- Log-on session
- Application

WHO

Online monitors will be reporting at regular intervals to operations and systems staff who can make use of the information to identify problems or potential problems and dynamically modify the system to optimize performance.

The information from historical monitors will be used by people who will use this information either for tuning or capacity planning. Capacity planners may even take the information as input for their modeling software in order to predict future requirements.

Written reports are usually sent to management and sometimes users.

Management

Management should be informed because they tend to view DP as "a bottomless pit of expenditure." Management may not clearly see what their money is buying and why more and more upgrade money is required. This is because they are typically informed only when severe problems occur or further upgrade money is needed. Often they do not see the DP staff as business-oriented, but rather as technicians who produce technical solutions and refuse user requirements.

This situation is clearly unacceptable. Any business depends on its information systems and vice versa; therefore, information must be regularly reported to management.

Users

Once service levels have been defined, it is important to ensure that they are being adhered to. This means producing reports for users to read on a regular basis. Successes should be publicized to prevent anyone being able to moan about DP's "continual failures."

WHAT LEVEL

Many online monitors will report whenever threshold limits are exceeded so that staff can immediately take the required steps to rectify the situation.

With historical monitors the reports produced on screen will depend on the requests made by the user, and the detail will depend on the depth of questioning. Historical monitor packages usually produce the results that are included in any written reports.

For written reports it is important not to swamp the recipient with information but to present only what is essential. The information should be clear and, as far as possible, nontechnical. The main areas that can be reported on are:

- Exception reporting on key values such as CPU utilization, paging, and response times.
- Service-level exploration by setting threshold limits reflecting the agreed service-level objectives and reporting on cases where the threshold is exceeded.
- Performance trends reports, showing degradation/improvement over a typical representative period.
- Workload growth forecasts: reports for workload and device usage for any given time can be extrapolated showing trends, and growth factors can be determined.
- Hardware growth projections: these should be based on the "what-if?" analysis wherever possible.
- Identification of system servers that are causing bottlenecks and any failure to meet the objectives.
- A report on how the business objectives can be met on the basis of the information available from the reporting tools should be produced.

It is worth stressing that recipients need only the information that is of value to them.

HOW PRESENTED

Any report must present the information in such a way that it can be quickly and efficiently understood. With software monitors exception reports can be highlighted or presented in a different color to draw attention to the information. A pile of paper an inch thick with columns of figures that all look very similar will probably take hours to read, and then there is only a small chance of identifying problem situations.

Ideally what is needed is graphic reporting so that problem situations can be spotted at a glance. Line graphs should be used to show variations of particular measures throughout the day, week, or month. Bar charts and pie charts can be used to show how various components of response time or utilization go to make up the whole.

SAS, with or without MXP, is used by many sites for the production of graphic reports. Others use their own graphics packages for generation of customized reports.

Reports should be produced to an agreed format at agreed intervals so that a quick appraisal reveals that all is normal or that problems have occurred. In the latter case further reports should be generated to focus on the problem in more detail and to isolate the cause and to suggest the best course of action to prevent future occurrences.

Status reports can be written using the following five headings:

- Problems identified
- Problems outstanding
- Problems resolved
- Activities/accomplishments
- Future plans

Users' perceptions of reponse times and turnaround times are often better represented by quantiles (e.g., 75th or 90th percentiles) than by averages. Users can usually understand the concept of a complex (as opposed to a trivial) transaction but will have expectations about both.

The use of graphs, color, and different fonts can highlight significant aspects of a report, making the information more easily digestible by the recipient.

HOW OFTEN

The frequency of reports depends on what use is to be made of them. For online monitors the report on screen may be updated every five seconds, for historical monitors the frequency can be controlled by the user. Management may require a brief daily written report highlighting any important events and a full, detailed report every week. Users may require a monthly report. Systems programmers may require a detailed daily report containing in-depth analysis of what happened the previous day, alerting them to any problems that may have occurred.

USE

Before any report is produced, the person producing it should always ask the same question: "Armed with the information contained in this, what is the recipient going to do?" If the answer is either "nothing" or "don't know," there is no point in producing the report.

The contents of a report need only cover those areas that the recipient needs to know. Otherwise the report writer is creating more work for himself that will go unread.

12

Tuning and Capacity Planning

Once the performance of the system has been accurately measured by using any of the performance monitor packages that are available or using a "home-grown" monitor and using any other sources of performance information available, it is necessary to make some use of all the data that has been accumulated. The data must be evaluated to produce information that can be used to identify system problems. From there, steps can be taken to eliminate these problems. This may take the form of "fire-fighting," "quick-and-dirty" modifications to the system, or may involve a reasoned approach involving planning for the future. The first method represents the worst approach to tuning, the other involves a combination of tuning and capacity planning. Measurement, evaluation, tuning, and capacity planning are all necessary components of performance management. This chapter examines these components and also looks at some of the issues surrounding installing a new system or upgrading an existing one.

MEASUREMENT

The first stage in any performance management process is the collection of data that accurately measures system performance. Measurement should not be restricted to information from a monitor, but should also include manual input from logs, records, and verbal communication with operators. It is useful to decide:

- What to measure
- How to measure it
- How the results are to be presented
- What is to happen to the results

EVALUATION

The second stage is the analysis of the results of the measurement. Any assessment of system load, contention, and system utilization will depend on the capacity of the system, its configuration, and the performance objectives that have been specified.

The load on the system can be defined in terms of the rate at which work arrives at a system resource. If the system were balanced, the rate at which work arrived would be equal to or less than the speed of the device. Work can be defined as a request for a particular function to be performed.

Contention is caused by work requests waiting for a resource to become available because other work requests are using it. This situation can be identified by a task taking longer to process than some "ideal" length of time. If a large number of tasks are waiting for a resource to become available, this is known as a bottleneck.

Utilization is usually specified as the amount of time that a resource is busy relative to the overall elapsed time. The figure is usually calculated as a percentage and may be used to specify threshold values for some monitors.

One area that might cause confusion is processor busy times. It should be remembered that the processor could be in supervisor state or problem state (i.e., processing work). Therefore, CPU utilization may not be a reflection of the amount of work that is being done.

The analysis of the measurement data should identify any bottlenecks or potential bottlenecks. This is the time to examine possible actions that may be required either to solve problems that have been identified or simply to improve overall performance. Where a bottleneck is identified, some action is necessary either to alleviate the bottleneck or to prevent it occurring. The four most common areas for bottlenecks are:

- CPU
- Central storage
- Paging
- I/O

It is a general rule that the removal of one bottleneck leads eventually to the identification of another one.

It is not always easy to identify which resource is the cause of a bottleneck because of the complex interrelationship of the four resources mentioned above. For example, a page-in operation will necessarily involve an I/O operation.

For this reason key areas must be monitored regularly. Trend recording is important, as deviations from the trend can be followed up immediately.

Any solutions will also have an associated cost that should be evaluated at this point to establish whether the gains will be worth the expenditure. This book contains suggestions for many areas that are worth examining. These include:

- Block size of disk files—increased sizes will reduce I/Os, but may increase the amount of storage used.
- The number of concurrent tasks may be reduced, or work rescheduled—this will reduce contention and paging rates and will consequently improve elapsed times for jobs.
- Files or mini-disks can be spread more evenly across devices, or read-only files or mini-disks can be duplicated—this should reduce contention on channels and devices and decrease overall wait times. Unfortunately, it may also require more storage devices, and with duplication there is a need for extra management to ensure all versions are updated at the same time.

TUNING

Tuning fits in as a natural part of performance management, with the objective of ensuring that hardware and software components perform according to specifications.

The first stage in any tuning exercise is to identify the system goals, i.e., to decide what type of work is to get the best service, etc. It may be that interactive CMS users are to get the best service, or it may be that a guest operating system running a large CICS network is to be treated most favorably by CP. Decisions like this must be taken right at the start and reevaluated at regular intervals in the light of management decisions on what is best for the company.

The purpose behind tuning is to optimize the overall performance of the system. However, the 80/20 rule will apply. This rule states that 80 percent of system performance benefits will be gained from 20 percent of the effort. Much time and effort can be wasted trying to tune the last 20 percent. Good tuning can put off the inevitable need to purchase new hardware, i.e., more main storage, faster I/O devices, etc.

It is worth trying to tune for what will be installed on the system as well as what already exists. It is also worth considering whether to tune for interactive users (Q1) or noninteractive users (Q2).

Tuning should alleviate or eliminate a bottleneck, although, as mentioned earlier, it will probably replace it with another constraint.

The golden rule for tuning is to make only one change at a time and measure what effect that one change has made to the way that the system performs.

There are a number of ways to tune a system. The following is a brief summary of some of the main categories (fuller details are given throughout this book):

- Upgrading hardware
- Changing parameter values
- File placement
- Rescheduling work
- Educating end users
- Rewriting application programs

Upgrading Hardware

Upgrading hardware is often a double-edged sword and should be used with care. A newer faster processor should be able to perform work faster and, therefore, do more in a day. However, if the previous system was constrained by I/O, a faster processor will not improve this and will probably make it worse.

If the previous constraint was paging, upgrading the hardware to provide extra main memory will reduce the amount of paging necessary and will improve overall performance.

All possible consequences should be considered before the expense of a hardware upgrade is incurred.

Changing Parameter Values

Changing parameter values can improve or damage system performance. For example, in Chapter 7 it was shown that with HPO systems the alternate channel is never used. If alternate channels are specified as the primary channel in the DMKRIO macro, it will help to reduce queuing in the channel, and so improve system performance. Other values in the various system modules can also be modified to enhance performance.

Other parameter values that can be changed are those following a SET command. These are discussed in more detail in Chapter 6.

File Placement

Chapter 7 examined in some detail the changes that could be made to optimize I/O. These included placing active files on disks at the end of strings, duplicating or caching heavily used read-only minidisks, and using 4K blocks. It was also suggested that files should be placed in order of frequency of use on mini-disks, and many other hints and tips are given.

Rescheduling Work

There are numerous examples at any site of activities that coincide causing contention and degradation in the response times observed. There are also typically long periods during the day when the resources available are underutilized or even completely idle. This is because the bulk of work is carried out during the standard 9 to 5 working day with peaks at around 10:00 A.M. and 02:00 P.M. It also means that from around seven in the evening until seven the following morning, very little of the machine resources are consumed. Wherever possible, applications should be rescheduled to avoid contention, and running as much work as possible out of hours is the obvious solution.

Another example is with the use of SQL databases. To improve performance and user response times, it is necessary to ensure that the statistics used by the optimizer when selecting data paths is up to date. The batch job updating these statistics cannot be run while users are on the system because it locks them out. The solution is to run it after hours, and a compromise solution, where required, is to run it during lunch breaks.

Educating End Users

End users may or may not have many misconceptions about what a computer is and how it works. However, their idea of how they want to use the system may not necessarily result in the best possible service being available for everyone else. End-user education can help to show them why they are asked to perform certain tasks and how it can impact on the other users. This education may change their attitude and ultimately their behavior.

Typical examples of end-user problems are: filling up the spool area with files that they no longer require, but have not bothered to delete; leaving a PROFS terminal switched on without using it for work; and accidently deleting live files.

Rewriting Application Programs

Many application programs still being used today are five or more years old. These programs may have been modified by a number of people over the years and may be carrying out all the work that is required of them, but they may be doing it in an unsatisfactory way.

If the program is to be rewritten, it is the ideal time to ensure that it makes use of any enhancements to VM or any improvements to the hardware that will improve its performance. It is also a good idea to reassess which is the best language for it to be written in, and to ensure all documentation about it is up to date so that future modifications will be less harmful in terms of performance deterioration.

Additional Considerations

The ideas given above are not all applicable to every situation, and the appropriate measure or combination of measures should be evaluated before being applied. The evaluation of potential solutions should include such factors as cost, delay before implementation, impact on other components, and how long the solution will last.

Cost   The cost of a solution has to be calculated. This might include the cost of new hardware, the overtime costs for staff to carry out the upgrade, or it may have to include the cost of new software, manuals, training, and overtime payments for staff to cover for those away on training courses. If new hardware is installed, there may be a requirement for new software to be purchased. The additional budget requirement may also be refused by the company so an alternative solution will have to be considered.

Delay   If a hardware or software component has to be ordered, there will be a delay before it can be delivered. This delay in solving the problem may be unacceptable and a more immediate solution sought.

Impact   If the performance of one virtual machine, for example, an SQL service machine, does not meet the required standard, it is possible to use SET commands to ensure that it gets better service from the scheduler and dispatcher. These commands include SET FAVOR, SET PRIORITY, and SET QDROP. However, the improvement in the performance of the one virtual machine will be at the expense of all the other virtual machines and thereby impact on the performance of the system as a whole. It must be decided whether this is acceptable.

Longevity   For the solution that is applied to the problem to be cost effective, it must last for a sensible period of time. If the solution is a stopgap to cover the period until new hardware or software can be delivered, then it must last for that length of time. If it is designed as a permanent solution, it must last for at least a year, preferably for three years. Too often quick-and-dirty solutions are applied. These eventually need replacing by sensible, well-thought-out strategies; otherwise, the system may come to a grinding halt.

The Never-Ending Cycle

Once a change has been implemented, it is time to start measuring and evaluating again to identify the next problem.

Avoiding Fine Tuning

Although it is apparently attractive, and usually a very high standard of technical work goes into such exercises, the fine tuning project typically costs far more in the end. These projects are often a response to inadequate hardware or some other unavoidable circumstance; however, the temptation to make the continued delivery of acceptable performance dependent on elaborate tuning should be resisted.

In fact, many believe that faced with the two alternatives, either a barely acceptable service which is easy to maintain or super performance which relies on ultrafine tuning, the former is the better choice. The most likely outcomes otherwise tend to be:

- Disaster resulting from a change usually caused by circumstances outside the programmer's control
- A very high degree of the complexity involved in effecting subsequent tuning changes

CAPACITY PLANNING

Capacity planning is usually considered to be "the provision of just enough resources, at just the right time, to handle a changing workload." It involves such aspects as:

- Planning for future growth
- Rescheduling work to avoid contention
- Producing reports

Capacity planning is dependent on:

- Accurate measurements
- Establishing and maintaining agreed service-level objectives

The ultimate objective of capacity planning is to ensure the following:

- The computer systems will do what is required of them when it is required of them
- Resources such as hardware, software, and staff are utilised efficiently
- A consistent service is provided by the computer system
- The computer services are provided to the business user at a justifiable cost

Planning

Planning activities are often triggered purely by problems, with the consequences that service levels are not maintained at satisfactory levels and users and customers are unhappy. With this general approach of reacting rather than acting, strategic directions are difficult to identify, and opportunities are often in danger of being missed by long implementation times.

The basis for any capacity management system is a formal, written capacity plan, produced according to the same rules as the formal annual budget. The senior management decisions are not necessarily concerned with what equipment to buy from whom, or whether to buy any at all, but with the quality and form of services to be provided to the business organization.

The capacity plan is an essential document in the management process of DP departments, and without it, it is virtually impossible for senior management to make any businesslike decisions in an orderly fashion.

The main benefit of a comprehensive capacity management system is that more time can be spent on the business analysis and forecasting; therefore, corporate business needs can be supported at all times.

To facilitate capacity planning it is usually necessary to build a model of the way that the system is currently performing and to use this model to predict what will be the effect of anticipated changes on the system. This is discussed in more detail below.

The capacity plan must include risk analysis.

Risk Analysis   Risk analysis is the analysis of the potential risks evaluated from the point of view of changes in business requirements, failures of components in the production resource, changes in vendor politics, and changes in funding.

Continual Capacity Planning

Having spent time and effort to produce a plan, it makes sense to follow up on the original exercise. Business plans evolve as the business evolves. Capacity plans must also evolve in parallel with the business evolution. Athough problems may have disappeared following a study, there is no guarantee that they will never recur. Therefore, constant monitoring is vital.

Pitfalls Management attention is often concentrated on the biggest, most expensive, or most politically sensitive component in the hardware configuration. One result of this is functional, performance, or capacity problems on minor peripherals, which may cause service problems that could have been avoided for a minimal investment.

Consequences When decisions about hardware solutions have to be made, the consequences are often far-reaching with expected return on investments spread over periods of four to six years or more. This means that solutions have to be selected so they can grow with future requirements. The life-cycle status of the equipment has to be determined so it does not become technically obsolete or discontinued before the end of the pay-back period. Ideally equipment should be field upgradable within this time frame.

Modeling

When planning for the future it is necessary to make some kind of estimate as to what the load on the system will be. This can be done by building a model of the system. However, there are two main problem areas in modeling: collecting all the data and calibrating the model. The amount of manual effort required to build models is substantial and in order to provide a fast, efficient, ongoing service to users, data collection has to be automated. Examples of products in this area are VM/PPF from IBM; CAPTURE/VM plus INFO/BASE and BEST/1 from BGS; CAPACITY/Q from Logica; SCERT from PSI; and finally parts of the SAS system from the SAS Institute. In more complex environments, e.g., VM/CMS/VSE/CICS, it is necessary to do more research and put more effort into collecting extra data to build accurate models. Many people tend to use the standard software monitors supplied by IBM to extract this extra data, but analyze the results by using SAS to bring information into a common format, for model building. Although this may take longer, it can be very successful.

Relevant Overheads

Historical data will reveal patterns in business trends, workload trends, and performance trends. It is therefore of great value both in tuning and capacity planning. The overheads are variable and will depend greatly on how much data is collected, how this data is controlled, and how it is meaningfully condensed. Overheads include time spent collecting data, evaluating it, and carrying out tuning and capacity planning exercises.

Cost Savings

Cost savings that can be achieved by capacity planning are very variable and really depend on the organization. A few examples of the types of cost savings that can be achieved are given below:

- A planned memory upgrade of 8 MB was shown to be unnecessary because the problem was due to priority levels.
- Refinements to an I/O subsystem improved its working so much that the purchase of two 3380 disks became unnecessary.
- A major hardware upgrade could be delayed by 6 to 12 months.
- The results from a study showed that a network's lines were oversized, which allowed for more terminals to be installed, and the purchase of new lines was avoided.

Managing New Applications

The technique of sizing new applications or systems (i.e., before implementation and, where possible, at design stage) is something that in the past has often proved to be unsatisfactory. Even if it was possible to give a reasonable forecast of the performance of a new application, it tended to be extremely difficult to prove the effect of this new application on existing computer systems.

Design mistakes are costly in terms of time, money, and credibility. Managers cannot afford to wait until a new program has been designed to find out if it performs as advertised; they need interactive tools to monitor system design at every step along the way.

When managing new applications, the key to productivity is time. Any modeling system that is used needs to recognize the delicate balance that exists between design time, production time, and delivery lead time.

Historically, applications and mainframe departments have looked at new online systems from different perspectives. Applications people are concerned with purchasing and designing new packages. Mainframe and network people are concerned with how those new packages will affect overall system performance. Managers must understand both perspectives.

There are many case histories of how an application that "looked fine" in development "brought the system down" in production.

Too often, new applications were sized in isolation, this sizing tending often to be erroneous. The application was then written and tuned on a development system, in perfect isolation. The system reached the point where it achieved its objectives (but still in isolation). Once put in production with other systems competing for common resources, disaster occurred and response times increased dramatically.

Key questions to be answered are:

• At what stage are performance requirements specified for new applications?
• Are performance requirements subject to rigorous testing prior to implementation?

In an ideal world, the capacity planner is intimately involved in every stage of the development process because he can have a valuable input to the design of applications, choice of language or database, etc.

SYSTEM SET-UP

Deciding on the set-up of a system really occurs in two major stages. There is the initial system set-up, and there is the system upgrade. In both of these situations performance management plays a key role, and system upgrade is often triggered by capacity planning decisions.

Initial System Set-Up

When the system is set up for the first time, that is the time to get everything right. Unfortunately, it is also the time when knowledge about the system is probably at its lowest.

A decision to install a system will have been made, and some decisions will be made as to what sort of demands will be placed on the system. However, these latter decisions will typically be wildly inaccurate and based on "guesstimates." Choice comes down to what hardware and software to install.

Hardware choices include:

- Which mainframe
- Which DASD
- Which network components

Mainframe Assuming that an IBM-type processor is selected as opposed to DEC or Unysis, etc., some of the questions to ask are:

- How many MIPS?
- How much does it cost?
  - Lease or buy
  - New or secondhand
  - IBM or PCM
- Is expanded storage required?
- Will the software selected run on it/use it to its full potential?
- Can it be upgraded?
- Which assists are available?

The choice of hardware may affect the choice of operating system. For example, if a 3090 is selected, only HPO or XA systems will run on it. Therefore, this rules out the selection of VM/SP as an operating system.

DASD For DASD some of the questions to ask are:

- How much?
- What capacity?
- Fixed or removable?
- FBA or CKD?
- Are solid state disks required?
- Will cache help?
- How many DASDs are required?

Again, hardware choices can affect software choices. If cache is required, it will not work with VM/SP.

Network For the network, similar questions apply:

- How much?
- What type of terminals are required?
- How many?
- Where are they to be located?

- How many controllers are needed?
- Leased lines/dial up?
- How many modems/what speed?

Other hardware requirements include printers, cables, and communications controllers, as well as power supply and air conditioning.

Software

For software the choice is even harder because there is a great deal of software available that perform similar functions. The choices include:

- Which operating system?
- Which subsystems?
- Which monitor?

Operating System   Assuming that an IBM operating system is required, the choice is VSE, MVS, or VM. Assuming VM is selected, the choice is which version of VM to choose. Each has its positive and negative aspects, and the choice must depend on business needs. Chapter 1 of this book briefly describes the different versions of VM and their use.

Subsystems   Again the choice is wide. CMS will come with VM, but other choices include:

- Guest operating systems (MVS or VSE)
- PROFS/PASF
- Database system
- CICS
- GCS/VTAM

The range is wide and will depend on the business needs of the company installing it. The choice of subsystem may affect the choice of operating system. For example, if MVS/SP is chosen, then HPO is often the best version of VM to use with it. Typically, VM/SP will carry too much of an overhead to make running MVS worthwhile.

Monitor To monitor what is happening on the system is very important, and the range of available monitors and capacity planning tools is mentioned earlier in the book.

Upgrade

Because a system that is performing well will attract more users, a time will be reached when performance levels fall below the required service levels and it is time to consider an upgrade. Upgrade paths can often be dependent on what was installed initially, and wrong decisions made at that time can lead to costly upgrades being necessary later. For example, if a processor at the end of its life in the product range was selected, it will be necessary to purchase a new processor, and the resale value of the old one may be greatly diminished.

Armed with information about the way the system has been utilized in the past, it is possible to predict with some degree of accuracy what future demand will be, and using this information it is possible to make the upgrade. This, like initial set-up, is the time to get it right. The advantage of an upgrade over initial system set-up is that the depth of knowledge will be greater and the probability of making the right choice is, therefore, much higher.

After an upgrade, it is important to ensure that virtual machines are exploiting any new facilities that have been included in order to improve their performance. It is also worth checking what facilities have been removed with the system upgrade and ensure that virtual machines are not trying to utilize them.

The opportunity to upgrade comes at irregular intervals. If capacity planning has been done well, it is possible to delay implementation for as long as possible and ensure that when it does occur all aspects will have been reviewed and steps taken to minimize the impact of the upgrade on customers and users of the system.

FUTURE PERFORMANCE IMPLICATIONS

At any upgrade, thought must be given to the impact in the future. Questions such as "Does the new processor allow an upgrade path?" and "Will IBM continue developing VM/SP HPO?" must be considered. No one can predict that a new application will be installed or how many new users will come onto the system, but any upgrade must contain some allowance for these and other contingencies.

The people responsible for performance management need to continually keep up to date with developments in the VM systems as supplied by IBM and their company's requirements of their system so that its performance is the optimum possible in their current situation and will continue to be so in the future.

1

Monitor Suppliers

This appendix contains the names and addresses of suppliers of VM monitors mentioned in the text.

Product	Supplier
ADABAS Performance Analysis System	Database Utility Group
BEST/1-VM	BGS
CAPTURE/VM	BGS
CMAP	VM/CMS Unlimited
CPWATCH	Waterloo tape
CRYSTAL	BGS
EXPLORE/VM	Goal Systems
MICS/VM	Legent Corporation
OMEGAMON/VM	Candle Corporation
SAS System	SAS Institute
SMART (VM/RTM)	IBM
SIM/SCOPE	Simware
Vital Signs	Blue Line Software
VMMAP	IBM
VM MONITOR	Systems Center
VM On-line Performance Monitor	Adesse

Product	Supplier
VMPRF	IBM
VPAC	Macro 4
Watch/VM	BMS
XAMAP	Velocity Software

Supplier Addresses

Adesse Corporation
36 Mill Plain Road
Suite 307
Danbury, CT 06811

BGS Systems, Inc.
128 Technology Center
Waltham, MA 02254

Blue Line Software
1500 S. Lilac Drive
Suite 340
Minneapolis, MN 55416

BMS Computer, Inc.
375 W. Wiget
Suite 210
P.O. Box 3086
Walnut Creek, CA 94598

Candle Corporation
1999 Bundy Drive
Los Angeles, CA 90025

Goal Systems International, Inc.
5455 N. High Street
Columbus, OH 43214

Legent Corporation
8615 Westwood Center Drive
Vienna, VA 22180

Macro 4, Inc.
Brookside Plaza
Mt. Freedom, NJ 07970

SAS Institute
SAS Circle
Box 8000
Cary, NC 27512

Simware, Inc.
20 Colonnade Road
Ottawa
Ontario
Canada, K2E 7M6

Systems Center
1800 Alexander Bell Drive
Reston, VA 22091

Velocity Software, Inc.
60 Alban Street
Boston, MA 02124

VM/CMS Unlimited, Inc.
161 Granite Avenue
Boston, MA 032124

2

Other Products

The suppliers of other software products mentioned in the text are given below.

Products that improve the VSE lock-file performance:

Product	Supplier
Cache Magic LF	SDI
Extend/VSE	Goal Systems
Softkey	Jeyco
Vlock/VM	Blue Line Software

Products that can be used for capacity planning:

Product	Supplier
CAPACITY/Q	Logica
INFO/BASE	BGS
SCERT	PSI

Products that can be used for communication:

Product	Supplier
CA-VTERM	Computer Associates
Multiterm	Blue Line Software
NETWORK DIRECTOR	Phoenix Systems

Products that can be used for communication (continued):

Product	Supplier
PASSPORT	MacKinney Systems
SIM/SESSION	Simware
SWITCH/VM	BMS Computers
TPX	Legent Corporation
TUBES	Macro 4, Inc.
VIRTUE	Westinghouse

Supplier Addresses

BGS Systems, Inc.
128 Technology Center
Waltham, MA 02254

Blue Line Software
1500 S. Lilac Drive
Suite 340
Minneapolis, MN 55416

BMS Computer, Inc.
375 W. Wiget
Suite 210
P.O. Box 3086
Walnut Creek, CA 94598

Computer Associates International, Inc.
711 Stewart Avenue
Garden City, NY 11530

Goal Systems International, Inc.
5455 N. High Street
Columbus, OH 43214

Jeyco
P.O. Box 5966
Lincoln, NE 68505

Legent Corporation
Two Allegheny Center
Pittsburgh, PA 15212

Logica Systems, Inc.
666 Third Avenue
New York, NY 10017

MacKinney Systems
2674A S. Glenstone
Suite 112
Springfield, MO 65804

Macro 4, Inc.
Brookside Plaza
Mt. Freedom, NJ 07970

Phoenix Systems, Inc.
3300 Northeast Expressway
Suite 4B
Atlanta, GA 30341

PSI Systems Corp.
P.O. Box 21
Pittsburg, KS 66762

SDI
1700 S. El Camino Real
Suite 501
San Mateo, CA 94402

Simware, Inc.
20 Colonnade Road
Ottawa
Ontario
Canada K2E 7M6

Westinghouse Electric Corp.
Management Systems Software
P.O. Box 2728
Pittsburgh, PA 15230

3

Hints and Tips

The following is a summary of the hints and tips given in this book.

Maximizing DPA Space

- The FSA should be kept to a minimum by:
  - Using the MIGRATE command to migrate unused page and swap tables (if using releases prior to 4.2)
  - Purging spool files to reduce the number of spool file blocks
  - Ensuring idle users log-off
  - Eliminating all unnecessary devices from user directory entries. This reduces the number of control blocks that occupy FSA space.
  - Numbering virtual device addresses consecutively to minimize the number of virtual channel and virtual control unit blocks
- The size of the trace table should be reduced (HPO 5 and above) by using the TRACE option of the SYCOR macro in DMKSYS, or the TRACE option of the SYSSTORE macro in HCPSYS.
- The size of the resident nucleus area should be minimized by:
  - Removing unwanted devices from DMKRIO
  - Removing modules from the loadlist that will not be used
- DCSSs should be used in DPA to reduce duplication of code.
- More main memory could be installed:
  - up to 16MB for SP

223

- up to 64MB for HPO
- up to 2GB for XA/SP
- The version of VM installed could be upgraded, e.g., a migration from SP to HPO or from HPO to XA/SP.
- The number of monitor buffers should be reduced using the BUFFS option of the SYSCOR macro—watch for monitor suspension records.
- The SET RESERVE command should be used sparingly.
- With XA the size of the V=R FREE area should be reduced using the VRFREE option of HCPSYS SYSSTORE macro.

Improving CP Performance

- The IUCV modules could be moved from pageable nucleus to resident nucleus.

Improving Paging

- With HPO, the SYSPAG macro should not be duplicated when new paging devices are added. Instead, new devices should be added to the existing macro.
- With VM/SP, if all the PAGE areas allocated are small, seek time is reduced and thus improves response time. One PAGE area should be allocated in the middle of a pack. If 3380s are used, size should be about 80 cylinders. When deciding on how many PAGE areas to set up, the general rule to follow is to allocate one per 3380 actuator for every 15 pages per second required. Paging packs should be allocated across as many control units and channels as possible to avoid contention. The SYSOWN macro should be used to specify CP owned volumes in an order that rotates the access around all the DASD paths.
- With VM/SP HPO, there is little point in trying to allocate more than one each of PAGE, SWAP, and spool areas on a pack because the additional one will not be used until the first one is filled up. PAGE and SWAP areas should be allocated in the middle of a pack, and kept small in size to reduce seek times. The recommended size for PAGE areas is 60 cylinders, for SWAP areas it is 120 cylinders. As many control units and channels as possible

should be used to avoid contention. The SYSPAG macro can be used to ensure that PAGE and SWAP areas are used in an order that rotates access around the different paths available. The default values for the SYSPAG macro should not be used.

- With VM/XA SP with XA, as with other systems, it is important to spread the load around as many channel paths (CHPs) as possible. The SYSCPVOL macro in HCPSYS can be used to specify the devices in the required path rotation order.
- The fastest devices available should be used.
- Fixed head devices or solid state devices (expanded storage or cache controllers) should be used for preferred paging space. This is because demand page-ins are carried out a page at a time, therefore, the overhead of DASD seek times and rotational delay significantly effect performance.
- Placing SWAP areas on DASD does not cause significant performance problems. This is because swapping involves blocks of pages, therefore, the DASD overhead is not so significant.
- The usual I/O tuning rules apply to paging and swapping devices. Enough devices and paths should be used to ensure good response. An extra consideration with swapping devices is that they should be spread over a number of channels to allow for simultaneous pre-paging of swap sets.
- TEMP areas should never be used for paging because of the deterioration in performance—although paging into the TEMP area will prevent the system from crashing.
- Expanded storage or cached 3880s are best used for page areas and 3380s for swapping areas. With HPO and XA, paging rates can be reduced by using expanded storage.
- PAGE space should be placed near the center of the disk, but should not be spread across the center. The center is considered to be zero and addresses run either side of it. If the PAGE area is either side of the center, seek time is increased.
- Paging and spooling always take precedence over other I/O. If S and Y disks are placed on the same packs as either paging or spooling, the response to CMS users will be much inhibited.
- If plenty of memory is available, there will be no paging. This in itself will improve performance.
- SP and HPO will perform I/O to the paging areas in the order that they are specified in the SYSPAG macro of DMKSYS. If multiple channels are in use, the specified volume names should alternate on a channel basis.

Improving I/O

- There are two advantages to placing heavily used software on a separate disk. (1) There is an improvement in performance. (2) It is possible to audit the use of the software. This is done by utilizing the VM accounting data.
- It is worth considering duplicating disks if the number of active users exceeds fifty. An example would be the CMS S disk. The duplicate should be from a DDR back-up so that all copies use the same shared S-STATs. The duplicate copy should be put on a different disk pack to avoid contention. A CMS Y disk must have the same Y-STATs. If the mini-disks are cached, it is often not worth duplicating them, provided that a high number of users are accessing them. Because the files will be continuously accessed they will stay in cache storage and so better performance will be achieved. With SP release 5, the more heavily used EXECs can be placed in shared segments. This relieves the strain on the Y disk, and improves access times to those EXECs.
- Heavily used mini-disks (for example, the CMS S and Y disks) can have their access times reduced if the files on them are placed in order. The order used should be based on frequency of use with the most heavily used file first. Although the exercise may be time consuming, the benefits are considerable. It is worthwhile doing it on a new disk so that the files are not fragmented—if this is possible.
- Allocating multiple mini-disks can be done using the directory. However, this is tedious and there is a software aid on the Waterloo tapes that will automate the procedure. The program is called "IPLER."
- Heavily used mini-disks will yield better performance if they are placed near the center of the pack and next to each other. This reduces the amount of head movement required to access them. It is also recommended that the minimum number of heavily used mini-disks are placed on any one pack.
- The best performance can be achieved if the busiest DASD volumes are placed at the end of a string. When a volume on a string is ready to be serviced, a flag is set at the volume. These flags are ORed together at the head of string. When it detects a service request flag, the head of string controller starts a sequential search of the string, checking to see which one requires service. When a flag is found, the controller services the volume and resets the flag. The controller will then return to the beginning. If the service request flag is still set, it begins the search again. If a heavily used

pack is placed at the beginning of string, it will tend to hog the service cycles and so lock out the trailing volumes waiting for service. If less heavily used volumes are placed at the start of the string, they will be serviced more quickly, and will be out of the path when the second scan is done.

- The 3380s A and D models were highly though of because of the amount of data that they could store. However, there is only one path available for the whole string. As the disks get busier, the likelihood of a busy head of string occurring increases. It is recommended that only one box (i.e., four addresses) on a string is used, and that a maximum of three be used.
- With model Es, Js, and Ks there are four paths to service a maximum of sixteen volumes on each string. Busy volumes should always be placed at the end of each substring, otherwise they will lock-out the less busy volumes.
- Because 3380 models A04, AA04, and AD04 have only one path to service up to 16 volumes, it is imperative that volumes are placed in the correct order in the string.
- With 3380 models AE04, AJ04, and AK04, there are four paths to each unit servicing four units in the string. Heavily used volumes should be placed at the end of the string.
- Heavily used strings should be placed lower on controllers, and heavily used controllers should be placed further down channels for similar reasons.
- Also, virtual addresses should be allocated in a similar way, because of the way that RDEVBLOKs are processed. Therefore, terminals should be on lower addresses than tape drives.
- An analysis of seek activity on a DASD can indicate highly used areas. A map of the allocated areas of the volume will show which virtual machine is responsible for activity against each area. Examination of the disk access analysis should be carried out at different times of the day because there may be a wide variation in the pattern of access and there is no point tuning for only one of several different access patterns.
- The SAVEFD command can be used to make file directories of common mini-disks shared. This save on I/O storage.
- It is never a good idea to put terminals on the same channels as paging packs. The service to the terminals will have to wait until disk I/O is complete.
- The heavy use of TDISKs can impact on I/O performance. Formatting is I/O intensive and can slow down other I/O activity.
- I/O activity needs to be balanced across devices, control units, and channels.

- System mini-disks should not all be put on one actuator, the load should be spread out.
- Actuators should be dedicated to PROFS DASD, i.e., they should not be shared with active data.
- The RECFM V parameter saves disk space, but RECFM F is faster.
- CMS mini-disks should be formatted using a blocksize of 4K.
- All the items on DASD should be cached, not just some. If some items are not cached, I/O takes place at normal DASD speed for that item. When I/O completes, cache speed I/O can take place. If only some items are cached, all the advantages of caching are lost.
- Page and data contention on the same channel should be avoided.
- A reduction in the number of I/Os carried out will improve overall performance.
- Dedicating DASD—this reduces the amount of translation work required by CP.
- If 3380s are not formatted into 4K blocks, a lot of space is wasted by the size of Inter-Block Gaps (IBG). No other number divides so exactly into the track size of a 3380 as 4K blocks do.
- The only reason for not using a 4K block size would be for mini-disks that contain very, very small files.
- CMS release 5, which has read ahead, will get 2 blocks during an I/O operation rather than just one. If 4K blocks are used, 8K will be transferred.

The real key to improving the performance of the network is to understand exactly what is going on. Additionally, four suggestions are given below that should improve a user's terminal performance.

- The SET REMOTE ON command as an XEDIT option could be used to improve response times on remote 3270 terminals.
- Entry Assist can be used to improve productivity when working at 3270 terminals.
- With HPO release 5, there are forward and backward options on the PF key retrieve (SET PF RET BACK/FORW). This can be useful to retrieve the previous command from the buffer.
- With HPO release 5, VTAM terminals can use the TERM BREAKIN GUESTCL command. This prevents XEDIT sessions from being interrupted by messages. The terminal will bleep, but remain in full screen mode.

Improving CMS

- Disks without any .MODULE, .EXEC, or .XEDIT macros are omitted from the CMS file search. Therefore, to speed up the CMS file search, data files should be kept on disk separate from MODULE, EXEC, AND XEDIT files.
- COMMAND or MACRO should be used as the file type for XEDIT macros.
- The SAVEFD command available with SP release 5 and above, can be used to make file directories of commonly used CMS mini-disks shared. This saves I/O and storage.
- The use of NUCXLOAD, EXELOAD, and shared segments will save program loads.
- Frequently used EXECs should be EXECLOADed. With SP release 5 and above, they can be placed in the installation segment (DCSSGEN). They can be shared in read-only mode by all users. This saves both time and storage.
- Faster alternatives to SORT and COPYFILE should be used wherever possible.
- GLOBALV should be used in preference to utility files to remember things across EXECs.
- The short ready message (R;) should be used instead of READY. This can be achieved by using the command SET READYMSG SMSG.
- The number of access disks should be kept to a minimum. This reduces the time and effort spent searching for a files.
- Files on the A disk should be stored contiguously and in the order of frequency of use, with the most frequently used files first.
- With XA SP release 2, CMS mini-disks and the user directory can be cached in expanded storage.

Improving REXX

- Appropriate items should always be enclosed in quotes.
- To avoid lots of unnecessary variables in large programs, DROP should be used.
- Internal subroutine calls are more economical than external ones.
- The ADDRESS command should be used. This saves the interpreter from having to perform synonym resolution or searching for EXECs of the same name before invoking a CMS command.

- EXECUPDT should be used to remove blanks and comments from EXECs, and CMPREXX for REXX. They can then be invoked much faster.

Improving ASM

- CMS I/O should be used because it is faster than I/O simulation.
- A branch to nucleus code is faster than SVCs.
- If external REXX modules are implemented as functions, they should be called RXFUNCTI.

Improving SQL

- Multiple SQL/DS databases should be installed in separate virtual machines, each with its own databases Other virtual machines should be allowed to communicate with it using IUCV.
- A DCSS should be used with multiple SQL/DS server machines.
- Two or three single thread server machines should be implemented if one is likely to become a bottleneck. This is easier than trying to split usage later.
- SQL should be used for query only activities as this is what it does best.
- LUWs should be kept small to reduce the amount of virtual storage required.
- SQL managed mini-disks should not be used as CMS mini-disks.
- Pool usage should be monitored to ensure that it does not fill up, causing a database abend.
- Data access paths are chosen by the optimizer, not the user, and may effect performance. Statistics used by the optimizer are gathered by running a batch job. Running the job may lock out users causing even worse performance.
- Statistics should be kept up to date.
- The clustered index option should be used.
- The number of indexes used should be kept to a minimum.
- Volatile data should be unloaded and reloaded frequently.
- The use of storage buffers should be maximized.
- The following modules should be made nucleus resident
      DMKIUA
      DMKIUE
      DMKIUL
      DMKBIO

- The SET QDROP dbname OFF USERS command should be used to enhance performance.
- Once SQL is up and running, the SET RESERVE command should be used.
- Automatic locking occurs much more often than expected.
- Users need to find out how to get around SQL/DS's many limitations.

Improving PROFS

- PROFS shared code should be put on a separate actuator from VMSRES.
- PROFS mini-disks should be given dedicated actuators.
- Two or three single-thread server machines should be implemented from the start, rather than trying to split usage when one gets overloaded.
- PROFS REORGS should be performed daily.
- Users should be educated to read and remove notes regularly, and to log-off when inactive.

Bibliography

CMS Performs. P. R. Ryall, May 1988. UKCMG, Monarch House, 1A Herschel Street, Slough, Berks, SL1 1SY, England.

Network Performance Management for IBM Users. May 1986. Various authors, Xephon, Newbury, Berkshire, England; WPWS, P.O. Box 4480, Winter Park, FL 32793, USA.

New Directions in VM. December 1987. Various authors, Xephon, Newbury, Berkshire, England; WPWS, P.O. Box 4480, Winter Park, FL 32793, USA.

Planning for Capacity. March 1988. UKCMG, Monarch House, 1A Herschel Street, Slough, Berks, SL1 1SY, England.

Software Performance Monitor. January 1987. Xephon, Newbury, Berkshire, England; WPWS, P.O. Box 4480, Winter Park, FL 32793, USA.

The Handbook of IBM Terminology. Jeff Hosier, December 1988. Xephon, Newbury, Berkshire, England; WPWS, P.O. Box 4480, Winter Park, FL 32793, USA.

VM and Departmental Computing. G. R. McClain, 1988. McGraw-Hill Book Company, 11 West 19th Street, New York, NY 10011.

VM Performance. November 1988. Various authors, Xephon, Newbury, Berkshire, England; WPWS, P.O. Box 4480, Winter Park, FL 32793, USA.

VM Performance in Practice. December 1986. Xephon, Newbury, Berkshire, England; WPWS, P.O. Box 4480, Winter Park, FL 32793, USA.

VM Software in Practice. January 1989. Xephon, Newbury, Berkshire, England; WPWS, P.O. Box 4480, Winter Park, FL 32793, USA.

VM Update. Various authors, Xephon, Newbury, Berkshire, England; WPWS, P.O. Box 4480, Winter Park, FL 32793, USA.

VM/CMS Commands and Concepts. Steve Eckols, 1988. Mike Murach & Associates, Inc., 4697 West Jacquelyn Avenue, Fresno, CA 93722.

VM/CMS Handbook for Programmers, Users, and Managers. Howard Fosdick, 1987. Hayden Books, 4300 West 62nd Street, Indianapolis, IN 46268.

Glossary

Addressing—Every page in virtual storage has an address. Without this there would be no way of keeping track of the location of pages. The address may be 24 bits long as in SP and HPO, or 31 bits long as in XA. Addresses are translated to give the actual location of any page. Every device attached to the processor also has an address; e.g., a tape drive might have an address of 481.

Address space—An address space is the name given to an area of virtual storage allocated to a virtual machine.

Address translation—If, for example, the address of the next instruction to be processed is 23447E and is outside the range of real storage addresses, CP will look up segment 23 in the segment tables. This will give the address of the appropriate page table. There it will look up page 4, which might give a virtual address of 67000. Therefore, the actual address of the next instruction is 6747E.

Advanced Program-to-Program Communication, *See* **APPC.**

APE—Application Prototype Environment is an APL-based system for prototyping applications in VM/MVS environments. It is primarily an Information Center tool (although IBM claims that it is appropriate for professional programmers).

APL—A Programming Language was introduced to promote Information Centers. It is powerful but consumes vast amounts of machine resource, needs a special keyboard, and is difficult to use.

APPC—Advanced Program-to-Program Communication is an SNA facility that allows program-to-program communication.

235

APPC/VM VTAM Support. *See* **AVS.**

Assembler—A very basic programming language, much favored by systems programmers in the past. It is still quite heavily used. Programs are assembled, rather than compiled, before execution.

AUTOLOG—During the VM IPL procedure it is usual to start a disconnected virtual machine called AUTOLOG. This can be used to initiate a number of commands in the correct sequence and so set up the VM environment without any intervention by the operator.

Auxiliary storage—This refers to storage outside the central processor complex, but electronically connected to it. Auxiliary storage contains the pages of virtual machines that are running under CP. It is formatted into 4K page slots.

AVS—APPC/VM VTAM Support is the VTAM version of TSAF and is available with VM/SP release 6.

Binary Synchronous Communication. *See* **BSC.**

Bottleneck—A constraint is caused by more requests for a service than can be satisfied. It can cause a degradation in system performance, e.g., long waits for I/O operations.

BSC—Binary Synchronous Communication is an older, slower, synchronous communication protocol.

C—Another programming language. It is part of SAA and preferred, by some, to Assembler.

CCS—The Console Communication Services feature of VM is used by VCNA to communicate with VM routines.

CCW—Channel Command Word is issued by the processor and used to give instructions to channels.

Channel Command Word. *See* **CCW.**

Channel-to-Channel Adaptor. *See* **CTCA.**

CICS/VM—A much cut down VM version of the Customer Information Control System, a multiuser transaction processing system.

CMS—Conversational Monitor System is the VM timesharing system. It is, technically, an operating system.

COBOL—A third-generation, much maligned, but still frequently used programming language. Rumors of its imminent demise have been circulating for many years; however, it continues to thrive.

Console Communication Services. *See* **CCS.**

Control Program. *See* **CP.**

Control Program Assist. *See* **CPA.**

Conversational Monitor System. *See* **CMS.**

Core table—A table that keeps a record of the contents of all the page frames within real storage (i.e., the page frame table).

CP—Control Program is the name given to the collection of software modules that make up the VM nucleus.

CPA—Control Program Assist is a microcode assist that helps guest operating systems run more efficiently under VM.

CTCA—A Channel-to-Channel Adaptor is used to link processors, allowing communication from a channel on one processor to a channel on another one.

Customer Information Control System. *See* **CICS.**

DASD—Direct-Access Storage Devices are used to store data on-line. They are typically disk devices.

DAT—Dynamic Address Translation is the name given to the process by which virtual addresses are converted to real addresses. The process necessary for virtual storage to be usable.

DBEXTENT—This is the SQL equivalent of a CMS mini-disk.

DBMS—Database Management System is a package that looks after the placement of data within a relational arrangement of records and the subsequent retrieval of information.

DBSPACE—These contain SQL tables and are located in DBEXTENTs.

DCSS—Discontiguous Saved Segment areas are used to speed up processing in VM. With shared segments space savings can be achieved by keeping a single copy of shared code in virtual storage.

DDR—DASD Dump Restore program is used to back up and restore data from disks.

Dedicated channel—A dedicated channel is one that is directly attached to a guest operating system. This avoids the need for VM to translate addresses of virtual devices.

Demand paging—The movement of pages into real storage following a page fault is called demand paging.

Direct-Access Storage Device, *See* **DASD.**

Directory—A file containing a list of all virtual machines and their characteristics.

DIRMAINT—DIRectory MAINTenance program is used to help with the maintenance of the system directory.

Discontiguous Saved Segment. *See* **DCSS.**

Dispatcher—The component of CP responsible for selecting for execution virtual machines from the queues.

Dispatch list—This contains those users competing for a time slice.

Display Management System. *See* **DMS.**

Displaywrite. *See* **DW/370.**

Distributed Systems Executive. *See* **DSX.**

Distributed Systems Node Executive. *See* **DSNX.**

DMKRIO—A CP module specifying the real I/O device configuration.

DMKSEL—This macro is used with HPO to select real storage pages for the freelist.

DMKSNT—A CP module containing system table names referring to saved systems, e.g., CMS, network control programs, 3800 data arrays, and national language repositories.

DMKSYS—A CP module that contains macros which affect VM performance e.g., SYSPAG.

DMS—Display Management System is an old product used to create ISPF type panels or menus.

DPA—The Dynamic Paging Area is part of main storage that contains pages from processing virtual machines.

DRCT—DRCT is an area on a CP-owned disk that contains the system directory. The directory contains the details of every virtual machine that can log-on to VM.

DSNX—Distributed Systems Node Executive is software that sits in a distributed machine (currently 370 or AS/400) to support unmanned data distribution across a network. The DSNX machine talks to a host machine running the DSX software. Typically DSNX is used to distribute software, updates, etc.

DSX—Distributed Systems Executive is an old product that provided central host library support, program dump, and batch data transmission among midrange systems (8100, Series/1, and System/36) connected in an SNA network. DSX on the host communicates with DSNX on a distributed node. The mainframe version of DSX was replaced by NetView Distribution Manager in May 1988.

Dump Viewing Facility. *See* **DVF.**

DVF—Dump Viewing Facility is the XA equivalent of IPCS.

DW/370—Displaywrite is a mainframe word processing package. It is used with PROFS.

Dynamic Address Translation. *See* **DAT.**

Dynamic Paging Area. *See* **DPA.**

ECPS—The Extended Control Program Support is microcode introduced to improve VM performance on medium-sized machines.

Eligible list—This is a list of virtual machines that would like to execute, but are not placed on the dispatchable list because of the current load on the system.

EVMA—Extended Virtual Machine Assist is a microcode extension to VMA.

EXEC/EXEC2—Before the introduction of REXX, within CMS there were these simple programming-like languages that could be used for, among other things, job control.

Expanded storage—An area within the processor complex that can be used with HPO and XA for paging.

Extended Control Program Support. *See* **ECPS.**

Extended Virtual Machine Assist. *See* **EVMA.**

Flushlist—This exists within the core table and contains pointers to pages that could be put on the freelist.

FORTRAN—A programming language more frequently used in scientific applications.

Freelist—This exists within the core table and contains a list of those page frames that are free for use.

Free Storage Area. *See* **FSA.**

Free storage extends—If the FSA fills up, it will take more space from the DPA. This reallocation of space is called a free storage extend.

FSA—The Free Storage Area is part of VM and allocated in main storage. It contains most of the control blocks used to control virtual machines.

GCS—The Group Control System is considered by many to be a cut-down MVS system that is run under VM so that VTAM can execute. A clumsy set-up.

GDDM—Graphical Data Display Manager is a mainframe package for creating and displaying graphic data on a terminal.

Graphical Data Display Manager. *See* GDDM.

Group Control System. *See* GCS.

Guest Wait State Interpretation Capability. *See* GWSIC.

GWSIC—The Guest Wait State Interpretation Capability is used by VM/XA for dedicated processors. The guest stays in SIE when in a wait state, and the dedicated processor appears to be 100 percent busy.

Handshaking—Handshaking is a method of giving a one-to-one match of guest real and guest virtual storage. This improves the performance of the guest system by reducing the VM overhead.

HCPSYS—The XA equivalent to DMKSYS.

High Performance Option. *See* HPO.

HPO—High Performance Option that is required to run MVS/SP guests successfully with SP. It contains many performance benefits over VM/SP.

Hypervisor—VM is often called a hypervisor because it is considered to be a superior form of supervisor software.

IFS—Interactive File Sharing is an obsolete system that allowed a few VSAM files to be shared under VM.

Input Output Configuration Program. *See* IOCP.

Interactive File Sharing. *See* IFS.

Interactive Problem Control System. *See* IPCS.

Interactive Productivity Facility. *See* **IPF.**

Interactive System Productivity Facility. *See* **ISPF.**

Inter System Facilities. *See* **ISF.**

Inter-User Communication Vehicle. *See* **IUCV.**

IOCP—Input Output Configuration Program is used to define to the processor the I/O configuration has available to it. It is very important with VM/XA.

IPCS—Interactive Problem Control System runs under CMS and is used for problem determination. It has been replaced by DVF in XA SP.

IPF—Interactive Productivity Facility is an old version of an ISPF type facility.

ISF—Inter-System Facilities is a package that allows up to four HPO systems to share mini-disks and spool files. It is essentially a rather crude attempt at providing the ability to create "clusters" of processors.

ISPF—Interactive System Productivity Facility is a menu driven facility that allows the novice user to get things done.

IUCV—Inter-User Communication Vehicle is used for the transfer of messages among virtual machines, or between CP and a virtual machine.

Logical Unit of Work. *See* **LUW.**

Look-aside entries—CMS reorders its list of nucleus resident functions so that the more recently used ones are at the top of the list and can be found more quickly and so improve performance.

LUW—Logical Unit of Work is the name given to the amount of work that is done between data alterations being committed (saved) with CICS or SQL.

MAINT—This is a monitoring and control machine used mainly by systems programmers.

MHPG—Multiple High Performance Guests were announced as being available with VM/XA SP. It supposedly allowed near native performance for up to six guest operating systems. The facility, which uses SIE assist, is incorporated in PR/SM on some 3090 machines.

Mini-disk—To allow each virtual machine running under VM to have its "own" disk packs, real disks are formatted into smaller units called mini-disks. The mini-disks can be allocated to the virtual machine and can have user files placed on them.

Module—A module is a nonrelocatable executable program stored on disk. When called, it is loaded into virtual storage and executed.

Multiple High Performance Guests. *See* **MHPG.**

NCCF—Network Communications Control Facility is a VTAM application providing network operator control facilities in SNA (and BSC) networks. NCCF provides the environment for other products such as NPDA, NLDM, etc. It allows a degree of automation of network administration through the use of command lists. It is now part of NetView.

NCP—Network Control Program is an SNA program resident in the communications controller (e.g., 3745). It communicates with the host through ACF/VTAM via a channel interface, and communicates with the terminals or another communications controller via TP lines. NCP off-loads certain line protocol and routing functions from the host CPU.

NETDA—Network Design and Analysis is a network development tool for SNA networks. It is written in APL and runs with GDDM.

NETPARS—Network Performance and Reporting System is a batch program for analyzing performance data collected by NPA or NPM.

NetView—NetView is an SNA network management product which includes some of the functions of NCCF, NLDM, NPDA, VTAM node control application, and NMPF. NetView 2.0 (June 1987) gives central management of distributed 9370s.

Network Communications Control Facility *See* **NCCF.**

Network Control Program. *See* **NCP.**

Network Design and Analysis. *See* **NETDA.**

Network Logical Data Manager. *See* **NLDM.**

Network Management Productivity Facility. *See* **NMPF.**

Network Performance Analyser. *See* **NPA.**

Network Performance and Reporting System. *See* **NETPARS.**

Network Problem Determination Application. *See* **NPDA.**

NLDM—Network Logical Data Manager is an NCCF application which collects SNA session-related information and makes it available to NCCF operators. It is useful in helping operators to detect network faults not explicitly picked up by other network management tools. It is now part of NetView network management software.

NMPF—Network Management Productivity Facility is now part of NetView.

NPA—Network Performance Analyzer is a performance monitor. It is now superseded by NPM.

NPDA—Network Problem Determination Application provides network error analysis. It requires NCCF to support it. It collects errors reported by communications controllers, modems, lines, cluster controllers, control units, and terminals, and organizes and displays error statistics. NPDA is now part of NetView.

NPM—NetView (was Network) Performance Monitor. Software for monitoring the performance (data flow, response times, etc.) of SNA networks. Data is transferred to the mainframe for analysis. It replaced NPA.

OfficeVision. *See* **OV/VM.**

OV/VM—OfficeVision/VM is part of IBM's new strategy for the office. It offers a single user interface to a number of existing products, i.e., PROFS, PASF, AS (Application System), and DW/370.

Nucleus—The necessary system programs for VM make up the nucleus. It is divided into the nonpageable nucleus and pageable nucleus.

Nucleus extensions—These are programs that help with the running of a VM system, but are not absolutely necessary. They can be identified using the NUCXMAP command. New extensions can be added using the NUCXLOAD command. They can be removed using the NUCXDROP command.

PAGE—An area allocated on disk for auxiliary storage. Virtual machine's pages are stored there while the virtual machine is processing.

Page—A virtual machine that is logged on will be allocated space in virtual storage. The space is formatted into 4K units called pages. When programs or data are copied from real to auxiliary storage or vice versa, they are moved in units of pages.

Page fault—A page fault occurs when the next instruction to be executed for an active program is contained in a page that is not currently located in real storage. The contents of the required page on auxiliary storage will be copied into a free page frame. Because the program cannot continue processing until the page-in takes place, it will be interrupted and another program will be processed.

Page frame—Real storage is formatted into 4K units called page frames. A reference to each page frame is maintained by the core table. A page of a processing virtual machine can be paged in from auxiliary storage to an available page frame in real storage.

Page-in/page-out—Copying the contents of a page from auxiliary storage to real storage is called a page-in operation. Copying the contents of a page from real storage to auxiliary storage is called a page-out operation.

Page slot—Auxiliary storage is divided into 4K page slots to contain the pages of virtual machines that are logged on.

Page steal—This is the name given to the process by which page frames that have been allocated to one virtual machine are reallocated by CP to another virtual machine.

Page tables—These are used to identify each of the 4K pages in a segment. They are pointed to by segment tables. After a page fault, the page tables are updated to reflect the new location of the page.

Paging—The process by which pages are copied to and from real storage page frames.

PASF—The PROFS Application Support Feature is a set of optional extras for PROFS. Many people feel that these extensions should have been included in the PROFS.

Passthrough—A piece of software that is used to enhance communication facilities with VM.

PERM—This is an area of the CP-owned DASD that contains CP nucleus, warm start, saved system, and error recording areas.

PMA—The Preferred Machine Assist is microcode that is available with VM HPO as a way of improving performance of guest systems.

PMAV—An enhancement to PMA allowed guest systems to improve their performance by its use.

Preferred Machine Assist. *See* **PMA.**

Privop—If a guest system attempts to perform a privileged operation (privop), an exception is taken and VM or microcode assists will simulate the effect of the privop.

Processor Resource/System Manager. *See* **PR/SM.**

Professional Office System. *See* **PROFS.**

Profile—All CMS users have a profile EXEC which is executed when they log-on. This can be used to set up PF keys and in general define their environment. There is also a profile XEDIT which can tailor a user's XEDIT environment.

PROFS—PRofessional OFfice System is the VM equivalent of a filofax providing services such as diary, text management, and messaging.

Programmable Operator. *See* **PROP.**

Program Status Word. *See* **PSW.**

Program Update Tape. *See* **PUT.**

PROP—PRogrammable OPerator is a VM facility that allows some automation of routine operator activities.

PR/SM—Processor Resource/System Manager allows the logical partioning of a single mainframe (3090E and above). Similar in nature to the Multiple Domain Feature of Amdahl hardware but utilizes the SIE assists.

Pseudo page fault—When a guest system is dispatching multiple address spaces or partitions, it will stop dispatching the active one on receipt of a pseudo page fault from VM and dispatch another one. This happens when a page fault has occurred for that partition.

PSW—Program Status Word is a double word (i.e., 8 bytes) that contains information about the current instruction being processed and the address of the next instruction to be processed. Unused bits in the second half of the PSW are set to zero.

PUT—Program Update Tape is a tape sent out by IBM with small enhancements and fixes for problems experienced by users.

PVM—Passthrough Virtual Machine is the Passthrough server machine.

Queue drop—When the runuser comes to the end of its allocated timeslice, it is called queue drop.

Queues—VM operates three dispatchable queues, usually referred to as Q1, Q2, and Q3. Q1 contains interactive users, Q2 contains long-term interactive users, and Q3 contains guest operating systems, typically.

Real storage—Real storage is the name given to the space available to processing programs within the CPU. It is made up of page frames. It is divided into a number of specialized areas including the Dynamic Paging Area. In more recent machines, with the introduction of expanded storage, it is called main or central storage. SP can only address main memory up to 16 Mb, HPO can address up to 64 Mb, and XA can address up to 2 Gb.

Remote Spooling Communication Subsystem. *See* **RSCS.**

Response Time Monitor. *See* **RTM.**

Restructured extended executor. *See* **REXX.**

REXX—Restructured EXtended eXecutor is effectively a combined programming and job control language. It is now part of SAA.

RMSIZE—This is used with HPO systems to specify in the DMKSYS SYSCOR macro the size of the DPA to be available above the 16-Mb line.

RSCS—Remote Spooling Communication Subsystem is a software component that allows VM to link to remote unit record devices, i.e., printers and card readers, and other spooling systems, e.g., JES2.

RSSIZE—This is used with HPO systems to specify in the DMKSYS SYSCOR macro the size of the extended V=R area.

RTM—Response Time Monitor is an optional hardware facility on some terminal control units. It collects ranges of response times for each device and can transmit this information to the processor, usually NLDM.

Runuser—The virtual machine in the dispatch list that is currently executing is called the runuser.

SAA—Systems Applications Architecture is a set of standard interfaces proposed by IBM to allow the portability of programs from one operating system to another.

Saved system—A saved system is a copy of the memory used by a system after it has been loaded. It can be IPLed by name, e.g., IPL CMS.

Scheduler—The component of CP responsible for organizing virtual machines into queues for dispatching.

S disk—The System disk for CMS users is maintained by the MAINT user-id, and all other CMS users have read-only access to it.

Segments—Virtual storage is divided into segments. Each segment is 64K in size except with XA, where they are 1024K in size. Segments are in turn made up of 4K pages. Pointers to segments are contained in segment tables.

Segment tables—CP must be able to address every part of real storage. The first part of the address uses the segment table. Within this are pointers to the appropriate page table.

Server (service) machine—A service machine is a virtual machine that can be used by any number of other virtual machines to access a facility. For example, SQL server machines will allow users to access one or more databases.

SFS—The Shared File System introduced with VM/SP release 6 allows file sharing at the file level rather than at the mini-disk level. Considered by many a great leap forward despite the additional overhead involved.

Shadow page tables—Shadow page tables are built by VM to map from guest operating system virtual addresses to real addresses.

Shadow Table Bypass Assist. *See* **STBA.**

Shared File System. *See* **SFS.**

SIE assist—The microcode enhances the way that VM/XA deals with guest operating system, and is used to make the MHPG facility work and also the PR/SM facility.

SIE—Start Interpretive Execution is a command available to VM/XA SP to initiate the execution of a guest system. It makes certain advanced facilities available and improves performance.

SIO—The Start I/O command is issued to initiate an I/O operation.

SIOF—The Start I/O Fast instruction allows the I/O request to be queued while the guest operating system that issued the request can continue processing other work.

SIPO/E—The System Installation Productivity Option/Extended was introduced to make installing new VM systems relatively simple.

SMART—The VM/RTM real-time monitor known as SMART gives online information about the state of the system.

SNA—Systems Network Architecture defines levels of protocols for communication between terminals, applications, and programs.

SolutionPac—Package of software providing (fairly) complete solutions for a specific application. SolutionPac Office Series attempts to integrate a range of products (e.g., menus have been made more consistent).

SPOOL—Part of the TEMP area is defined as SPOOL. This stores users' print, punch, and reader files.

Spool files—Spool files are stored in the SPOOL area and can fill it up causing performance problems. Spool files can be reader, printer, or punch files.

SQL—Structured Query Language is a standard for access to relational databases, in particular SQL/DS.

SQL/DS—The most frequently used database with VM is SQL/DS. SQL/DS stands for Structured Query Language/Data System.

SRM—System Resource Manager is software responsible for the optimization of work throughput and resource usage.

SSCH—The Start SubCHannel command is issued with XA systems by the processor to initiate activity in a subchannel.

Start Interpretive Execution. *See* **SIE.**

STBA—Shadow Table Bypass Assist is a microcode feature that improves the performance of guest operating systems that dispatch more than one address space.

Structured Query Language. *See* **SQL.**

Structured Query Language/Data System. *See* **SQL/DS.**

SWAP—With HPO, areas on disk can be allocated as SWAP areas. These are used for swap sets.

Swapping—With HPO, swapping was introduced. In this process a block of pages is moved from real storage to auxiliary storage (swap-out) or from auxiliary storage to real storage (swap-in). This process usually improves overall performance.

Swap sets—The working set pages of individual users are grouped together to form swap sets which are then swapped in and out of real storage to SWAP areas on DASD.

Swap queue—With HPO, swap queues exist for interactive and noninteractive users. Users on the swap queue may have their pages swapped out.

Swap tables—These describe where on disk a user's pages are, if that user has been swapped out.

SYSCOR—The SYSCOR macro specifies the maximum real storage size that VM can utilize.

SYSGEN—SYStem GENeration is the name given to the process by which new operating systems are produced to run at a particular site.

SYSJRL—The SYSJRL macro is used to specify journaling options that can be used to record resource usage.

SYSMON—The SYSMON macro is used to specify the parameters to be used when collecting performance monitoring data.

SYSOPR—The SYSOPR macro is used to specify the user-ids of the system operator and the user to receive a system dump in the event of a restart.

SYSOWN—The SYSOWN macro is used to specify the CP-owned volumes. These volumes contain the PERM, TEMP, DRCT, and TDSR areas.

SYSPAG—The SYSPAG macro in DMKSYS specifies parameters to be used in paging and swapping.

SYSRES—The SYSRES macro is used to set up the IPL volume, specifying the unit address and device type, and also areas for the nucleus programs, error recording, and warm start areas.

System Installation Productivity Option/Extended. *See* **SIPO/E.**

System Resource Manager. *See* **SRM.**

Systems Applications Architecture. *See* **SAA.**

Systems Network Architecture. *See* **SNA.**

TDSK—An area on CP-owned DASD that can be used by virtual machines for the creation of temporary mini-disks.

TEMP—Space on the CP-owned DASD used for spooling and paging is allocated as TEMP space.

Thrashing—Thrashing is the name given to the state in which the system will steal pages to accommodate the working set of one virtual machine only to find that it almost immediately needs to page-in some of those pages that had been stolen. It will then repeat the process of stealing and paging. The system spends a lot of time in supervisor state carrying out the process. As a result of this, response times for the virtual machines will deteriorate. It is a clear symptom of performance problems.

Timeslice—The unit of time allocated for the processing of virtual machines. The length of the timeslice depends on the processor type.

Trace table—The trace table is located in real storage and stores information about events in a wraparound manner. It can be used to identify system problems. With HPO and XA its size can be reduced.

Transient area—This area is 8K in size (addresses E000 to FFFF) and can be used to store nucleus extension programs that can be invoked from the user area without affecting the user program in any way.

Transparent Services Access Facility. *See* **TSAF.**

Trimming—The process by which pages from the working set of a user that have not been referenced and have not been placed in a swap set are placed on the flushlist is called trimming.

Trim set—With HPO, those pages that are in main storage, but have not been referenced at queue drop time, and are not included in the swap set are considered to be part of the trim set. These pages are put on the flushlist.

TSAF—Transparent Services Access Facility is the peer-to-peer network software that runs under VM. It provides transparent user access to multiple 370 devices.

TTIME—TTIME is the total time taken for a guest system to complete a piece of work. It includes the VM supervisor time.

TVRATIO—The TVRATIO is used as a measure of the VM overhead for guest systems. It is the ratio of TTIME against VTIME.

V=F—With XA, up to five guest systems can be run Virtual=Fixed, which offers some of the advantages of V=R working.

V=R—It is customary to run MVS guest systems in real storage. This is written as Virtual=Real.

VCNA—Virtual Communication Network Application is the old version of VSCS.

Virtual address—An address that refers to either virtual storage or to a virtual I/O device. This address must be converted into a real storage or I/O device address when it is used.

Virtual Communication Network Application. *See* **VCNA.**

Virtual device—A virtual device is one that appears to be attached to a virtual machine. The real devices are shared so that the virtual devices can be used. There are control blocks associated with the virtual devices that are kept in main storage. The virtual devices associated with a user are specified in the directory.

Virtual Interval Timer Assist. *See* **VITA.**

Virtual Machine Assist. *See* **VMA.**

Virtual Machine Communication Facility. *See* **VMCF.**

Virtual RSCS Network Application. *See* **VRNA.**

Virtual storage—Virtual storage is the name given to the storage space available to logged-on virtual machines that appears to be in the CPU. In fact, to accommodate more virtual machines than would otherwise be possible, virtual storage is on disk or another medium outside of the real storage part of the processor. Virtual storage spans real storage and auxiliary storage.

Virtual Telecommunications Access Method. *See* **VTAM.**

VITA—Virtual Interval Timer Assist is a microcode assist that was important for older operating systems running under VM to improve their performance.

VM—Virtual Machine.

VMA—Virtual Machine Assist is a microcode assist that helps the performance of guest systems.

VMBLOK—This control block contains detailed information about each virtual machine that is logged on to VM, including its user-id.

VMCF—Virtual Machine Communication Facility allows data to be sent and received between virtual machines.

VMDBK—This is the XA equivalent of the VMBLOK.

VM/DSNX—VM Distributed Node Executive. *See* DSNX.

VM/IS—Virtual Machine/Integrated System is an easy-to-install version of SP used on small systems.

VM/ISF—VM Inter-System Facility. *See* ISF.

VMMAP—VMMAP is a historical monitor available with SP and HPO versions of VM. It will produce reports of what has happened to the system.

VM/MHPG—VM Multiple High Performance Guest. Multidomain feature running under VM/XA. Superseded by PR/SM on 3090E models.

VM/PPF—A performance planning facility (or performance modeling tool) that is available with VM.

VM/PRF—The VM Performance Reporting Facility works with VM/XA to produce reports on resource usage. It is similar in function to VMMAP.

VM/RSP—VM Remote System Programming Support. Remote support service provided for VM/IS installation.

VM/RTM—Real-time monitor which is better known as SMART.

VM SNA Console Support. *See* **VSCS.**

VM/SP—The basic version of VM (System Product) that is used on small and medium systems.

VM/SP HPO—The version of VM with the High Performance Option that is used on larger systems with MVS as a guest system.

VM/XA SF—The System Facility version of VM/XA will support MVS/XA as a guest, but requires a VM guest to provide the functions associated with VM.

VM/XA SP—A full-function version of VM utilizing 31 bit addressing and giving up to 2 Gb of storage. The other advantages of VM are available.

VRNA—Virtual RSCS Network Application is a set of add-ons to RSCS release 2 that allows data to be routed to applications under non-VM operating systems.

VSCS—VM SNA Console Support allows applications from SNA terminals to access VM. It runs under GCS.

VTAM—Virtual Telecommunications Access Method. This runs under GCS to allow SNA communication.

VTIME—The time taken for a guest system to complete an operation. It does not include any time spent by VM.

Working set—The working set of a virtual machine is the page frames in real storage that it has allocated to it or that it will require to have allocated to it in order to process. The working set size required for a virtual machine is recalculated at queue drop time.

XEDIT—eXtended EDITor for CMS users. It is a very comprehensive and much-loved editor.

Y disk—The Y disk is used by all CMS users in read only mode. It contains files that are maintained by the MAINT user-id.

Index

Throughput analysis, networks, 146–147
Trace table
  contents of, 18–19, 45
  default size, 45
Transfer in channel, Channel Command
  Word, 113
Transparent Services Access Facility,
  141
Trimming, 54
Trim set, 54
Tuning, 201–206
  cost aspects, 205, 206
  end user education, 204
  file placement, 203
  hardware upgrade, 202
  longevity of system, 205
  parameter values, 203
  purpose of, 202
  rescheduling work, 203–204
  rewriting applications, 204
TVRATIO, use of, 13–14
Upgrade, aspects of, 213
VBBLOK, 16
VCHBLOK, 16
VCUBLOK, 16
VDEVBLOK, 16
Virtual Communication Network
  Application, 140
Virtual equals real, 57
Virtual Interval Timer Assist, of ECPS,
  71
Virtual Machine Assist, 68–70
  and CMS, 70
  instructions used, 70
  MICBLOCK, 68
  privileged operations, 68
  shadow page tables, 70
  VMA CP relationship, 69–70
Virtual Machine Communication
  Facility, 141
Virtual machines
  address, 42
  core tables, 42
  demand paging, 40
  multiprocessing, 40
  multiprogramming, 40
  page stealing, 40–41
  page tables, 42
  segments, 42
  swapping, 42
  swap tables, 42
  thrashing, 41
  working sets, 40, 47
Virtual storage
  auxiliary storage, 39–40

Conversational Monitor System,
  152–155
Customer Information Control
  System, 160–163
guest operating systems, 155–160
PRofessional OFfice System,
  166–167
Structured Query Language/Data
  System, 163–164
Supervisor state, 13
Suspend/resume channel programs, 55
Swapped out users
  paging, 54–55
  processing of VM, 37
Swapping
  HPO swapping, 62–63
  of virtual machine, 42
Swap queues, 51
Swap sets, 54
Swap set size, freelist, 51
Swap tables, of virtual machine, 42
SWPTIME, use of, 83
Synchronous data link control, 137
SYSCOR macro, 22
SYSCOR TRACE, 45
SYSGEN, 22
SYSJRL macro, 23
SYSMON macro, 23
SYSOPR macro, 23
SYSOWN macro, 23
SYSPAG macro, 23
SYSRES macro, 23
System modules, 21–24
  DMKRIO, 21
  DMKSNT, 21–22
  DMKSYS, 22–24
System Resource Manager, SET
  commands
  APAGES, 83
  DSBUF, 84
  IABIAS, 84
  IBUF, 83
  LDUBUF, 84
  MAXPP, 83
  MAXWSS, 84
  MINNUMSS, 83
  PGULL, 85
  PREPAGE, 84
  STORBUF, 84
  SWPQTIME, 83
TDSK area, contents of, 26
Telecommunications network, in
  network, 137
TEMP area, contents of, 26
Terminal, in network, 137–138
Thrashing, of virtual machine, 41